Going All The Way

Going All The Way

♦

The Heart and Soul of the Exceptional Marriage

Brian Gleason LCSW and Marcia Gleason LCSW

iUniverse, Inc.
New York Lincoln Shanghai

Going All The Way
The Heart and Soul of the Exceptional Marriage

Copyright © 2007 by Brian Gleason

All rights reserved. No part of this book may be used or reproduced by any means, graphic, electronic, or mechanical, including photocopying, recording, taping or by any information storage retrieval system without the written permission of the publisher except in the case of brief quotations embodied in critical articles and reviews.

iUniverse books may be ordered through booksellers or by contacting:

iUniverse
2021 Pine Lake Road, Suite 100
Lincoln, NE 68512
www.iuniverse.com
1-800-Authors (1-800-288-4677)

Because of the dynamic nature of the Internet, any Web addresses or links contained in this book may have changed since publication and may no longer be valid.

The information, ideas, and suggestions in this book are not intended as a substitute for professional advice. Before following any suggestions contained in this book, you should consult your personal physician or mental health professional. Neither the author nor the publisher shall be liable or responsible for any loss or damage allegedly arising as a consequence of your use or application of any information or suggestions in this book.

ISBN: 978-0-595-45151-7 (pbk)
ISBN: 978-0-595-89460-4 (ebk)

Printed in the United States of America

To our parents,
Charles and Lillian,
Marie and Jim,
for teaching us the meaning of commitment.

Contents

Acknowledgments . . . . *ix*
Introduction . . . . *xi*
Why Marriage? 1
What Do We Want? 6
Too Much Thinking 12
Energy and Emotions 23
The Four Stages Leading to the Exceptional Marriage 36
Full Self Expression 69
Marriage Mentoring 100
Afterword *115*
Bibliography *117*
About The Authors *119*

Acknowledgments

A shout out goes to all those couples who have graced us with their honesty, vulnerability, and most of all, their indomitable spirit that they have shown in the face of strong and scary emotions. You have taught us much. We also bow to all our teachers, healers, guides, and therapists who, over the years, have helped **us** discover more and more of who we truly are.

Finally, to all the mentor couples who have trusted us and supported our vision. You know who you are, but we will proclaim your names just the same. Marsha and Michael Antkies, Judy Gotlieb and Neal Brodsky, Margot Harris and Craig Thurtell, Marian and Frank Schnecker, Irene Humbach and Dave Rider, Brenda and Doug Hantman, Sally Schwager and Eric Lifgren, Miranda and Peter Black, Sandie and Gerry Rumold, Liz and Barry Carl, Marlene and Bob Neufeld.

Introduction

o o o o o o o o o o o o o o o o o o o o o o o o o
Tranquility in love is a disagreeable calm.

—*Molière*

It is doubtful that there is anything in our world so desperately sought after and so intensely resisted as the long-term, committed relationship. The thing that we want most, we know deep in our bones, requires the most of us. Many sign up, but when the challenges arrive, as they always do, few dare to go all the way. Paradoxically, a relationship offers safety and security nestled alongside danger and risk. It feels risky to give yourself fully to another. If it's mere comfort you are seeking in your relationship, however, you are overlooking its profound potential.

This book is for all of you in committed relationships. Its purpose is to help you use your commitment, your relationship to make life better. One of the great gifts of marriage is the potential to discover all of who we are as individuals. The emotional allegiance forged between you and your partner is the basis for a lifetime's worth of personal growth and fulfillment.

You don't have to search any further than the person you are spooning as you lay in bed at night. Nearly everything you want to know about yourself, your relationship, intimacy, success, pleasure, and even spiritual awakening is accessible through the crucible of your marriage. The problem is that most couples sink down into emotionally numbing habits of interacting and opt for marginal connection and a glass of warm milk. As a result they miss the most significant of all their wedding gifts: the gift of fulfilling each person's great potential. The secrets of life do not require esoteric practices or sojourns to sacred Himalayan retreats. They are here in your relationship, waiting to be revealed.

My wife Marcia and I met in 1976, and two years later, we exchanged our vows. Now, three decades hence, we are still finding our way together through this often baffling and always precious experience of life. In the intervening years, between disco and hip-hop, we gradually found ourselves drawn deeper into the exploration of a life fully shared. What is written in these pages reflects our shared understanding of what marriage is meant to be. We use the term marriage to signify a long-term, committed relationship, and we recognize that what we suggest here may apply to many of you who for various reasons do not or cannot possess a marriage license.

It's our desire in this little book to get you to examine and understand:

A. How your relationship can and should be the most transformative and powerful experience of your life; and
B. Why it so often falls short of your expectations.

There has been so much written about how our pasts influence our intimate relationships, but relatively little about what we may become—that is, our potential. Much of the focus in couple's therapy can be characterized as "divorce prevention," which emphasizes the bottom end of marital relationships. As necessary as this is, we all need a model of how to maximize the potentialities inherent in the committed relationship. This book offers some suggestions for building a marriage that can be the catalyst for creating what we long for. What Marcia and I call "the Exceptional Marriage" is one in which both partners support each other in fulfilling their respective human potentials.

Marcia and I have watched with sadness the breakup of far too many marriages among friends, family, and colleagues. Some hid their struggles well. For others it was abundantly clear that they were resigned to going through the motions. Too often we have witnessed couples who have entered marriage with wide-eyed optimism be reduced to myopia in vision and heart. The tangled path from "I do" to "I didn't" is marked by many crossroads where couples repeatedly choose to avoid the emotionally uncomfortable options. Instead of expressing their hurts, fears, and angers, they withhold. Years or decades of withholding lead to an emotionally brittle relationship infused with bitterness and congealed resentment that leaves partners unable to be touched by each other.

Over time, when partners fail to engage in the necessary conflicts that intimacy requires, the cumulative resentments calcify into an impermeable hardening of the heart. As marital therapist and author David Wile (1993) describes it, "It is the adjustments, accommodations, and sacrifices that partners make without telling each other or fully recognizing it themselves—that is, their automatic and unverbalized attempts to compromise and be reasonable—that may lie at the root of the difficulty. What these partners may need is to stop compulsively compromising and to develop an ability to complain."

Marriage is supposed to be the holy terrain of all things intimate. With our spouses as in no other relationship, we are invited to share our most private places—our desires, fears, fantasies, and passionate emotions. But this often fails to blossom. Why? Because in large measure, strong emotions remain in the closet.

Most relationships slip into stale habits of interaction that skirt the places of our greatest vulnerability. When we feel most vulnerable, those places inevitably link to our need for each other. The recognition of our need for our partner evokes powerful feelings. Need brings with it fear of loss, hurt due to rejection, and anger from insult. We are fundamentally feeling creatures, and we have too often forgotten how to feel. Without a willingness to have all our emotions—difficult and pleasurable—we cannot go all the way.

Intimacy is not safe; it is a most risky venture indeed. Nor is it gentle, polite, or politically correct. True intimacy is a florid expression of the entire range of human emotions. Marriage is its container and the place where we can be ourselves. Unfortunately, we live in an age increasingly wary of potent emotional expression. In our quest to make relationships cruelty free and safe from violence, we have gone too far and euthanized passion. One thing has become abundantly clear in our work together: marriages and long–term, committed relationships suffer most from the squelching of passion and life force. These are the very attributes marriage ought to be cultivating.

In particular, anger has received a bad rap as the sultan of negative emotions. Anger-management programs have proliferated as a means to stem the tide of domestic violence. As full-fledged human beings, we don't need to manage anger any more than we need to manage sadness or love. The cover story of a renowned New Age magazine recently offered this headline: "The Courage to Do Nothing: An antidote to anger and other strong emotions." At what point did aggression become a disease, a perverse quirk of human nature, a plague? Anger is not anthrax. It needs no antidote. It is a force that can call forth abundant energy and vitality in a committed relationship. It is a natural response when we feel our attachment to a loved one is threatened. As Emerson once put it, "Sometimes a scream is better than a thesis."

It's not that anger can't be dangerous or that we don't need to employ reason and will to make choices that cause no real harm. But what Marcia and I have learned in our work with couples is this: Most marriages perish from atrophy, not from conflict. They suffer the grinding fate of emotional starvation, not the conflagration of unfettered emotional outbursts. The end result is that couples settle into controlled patterns of relating, or they drift toward some anticlimactic conclusion. They tell themselves, "I guess this is as good as it gets," or, "We just don't love each other anymore."

The essence of this book is about learning to express ourselves more fully to our partners. This means claiming one's feelings, not just learning techniques to communicate more effectively. After all, marriage is not a negotiation or a deal to be hashed out. It is the vehicle for achieving that which we hold most dear: our love, authenticity, and creativity.

Sadly, couples too often hide behind resentments, icy detachment, or Herculean efforts to remain unaffected by one another. In bad marriages, simmering hostility permeates the fabric of daily life. Silent disdain morphs into bickering, blame, and resignation from possibility. Nobody's willing to express from their souls how truly awful it has become.

In good marriages there is security, affection, compatibility, and warmth. Such couples enjoy a certain contentment while brushing aside or relegating to fantasy life the juiciness of passion. It is the exceptional marriage that refuses to settle for mere warmth. Such couples like it hot.

We are going to make the case for a more open, honest, passionate, and sometimes unpredictable expression of the wide and glorious range of human feelings. We are going to describe to you why this is so vital to intimacy and exactly what is involved in expressing ourselves openly. We are going to ask you to reevaluate your scripted notions of life in a committed relationship. We want to instill in you a sense of what is possible in your marriage.

Nearly all couples, including Marcia and me, learn to control the flow of feelings to protect ourselves from the scary places. We are frightened to let loose all those parts of us that might be scoffed at, ridiculed, held in contempt, rejected, abandoned, or even harmed by the one to whom we have committed our lives. So we neuter our passion and stifle our creativity. Yet the exceptional marriage is exemplified by taking risks—by latching on to the tiger's tail and going on a wild ride. In doing so, we discover our potential.

Why Marriage?

o o o o o o o o o o o o o o o o o o o o o o o o

Love is the extremely difficult realization that someone other than oneself is real.

—Iris Murdoch

Attempting to clearly define the long-term, committed relationship is akin to describing the ocean through chemical analysis. Like the ocean, marriage is deep, wide, ever-fluctuating, and filled with wonder and treachery. It is not reducible to psychological, social, biological, or even spiritual definitions. We are best served here by embracing a wide array of perspectives. How does the scientist view the ocean? How about the sailor, the poet, the child? Marriage, like the old breakfast commercial proclaimed, is magically delicious. It is also unfathomably unpredictable and unimaginably challenging.

Why do so many of us embark on the voyage across the sea of commitment? The vast majority of us seek out this union of body and soul without ever grasping why. Every marriage commences with the promise of mutual happiness, but we cannot possibly imagine what we are in for. The fact that a life-long commitment will probably be the hardest, most challenging undertaking we ever sign on for escapes us at the outset.

We are all too familiar with the problems associated with long term commitment. From the minor annoyances of personality quirks to the challenges of monogamy, from the pressures of responsibility for another human being to the vulnerability associated with rejection, criticism, betrayal, or loss, we sign on for this most risky of endeavors. In the cold light of reality, it can seem impossibly daunting.

None of this appears to matter, though, as we humans continue to choose marriage as the preferred lifestyle. There are psychological, biological, romantic, social, and spiritual theories to explain why marriage is so predominant in our world. We are marrying our parent. We are fitting in. We are creating a legal union that protects us and serves our financial interests. We are soul mates. We are creating a family unit for the benefit of raising children and perpetuating the species. We are madly in love. Such are the explanations put forth as to why people marry.

Our desire is to shine a light on the great potential inherent in marriage. To live so intimately for so long with this one other person (even as kids come and go) offers us an unprecedented opportunity to examine the very fiber of our being. Only in marriage will you have to face yourself in all your glory and ignominy. Marriage is the marathon of adult human development. Within its boundaries, each of us will test the mettle of our character. It can bestow upon us both peak and abyss experiences. Through the crucible of commitment, we are offered a unique chance to find out who we truly are—and then to become even more than we imagined. To take advantage of this enormous gift is the defining quality of the Exceptional Marriage.

The sacredness of marriage is embedded in the mundane. Through the nitty-gritty of every day life, we will encounter the greatest opportunities to find out who we are. The human spirit unfolds in the context of shared experience. How do we handle sickness, differences in child rearing styles, sexual insecurities, money, envy, holidays, ageing, and making the same damned mistakes over and over? When we are exposed to each other's idiosyncratic ways on a daily basis, we find the stuff of growth.

In marriage, we choose the person with whom we will share the bulk of our adult lives. This happens in no other relationship. We are born to our parents, and we accept the child who is born to us. Only in marriage do we have the privilege of picking each other. What a privilege! What a breathtaking, adrenaline-elevating responsibility! Each day, we wake up next to this other human being who has opted to climb into the same bed as us night after night after night. We can hardly begin to grasp the profundity of this decision. And we make this decision (whether we are aware of it or not) every single day. I choose you this morning, and this morning, and this morning.

The specialness of this circumstance can scarcely be overstated. Marriage, as a human endeavor, stands alone in this regard. No other form of relationship provides quite the opportunity or quite the challenge that marriage bequeaths. In these pages, we hope to help emancipate marriage from the limits that have inhibited its potential.

Couples rein in the possibilities afforded them in the committed relationship for multiple reasons, many of which we explore in the coming chapters. For now, we will say that the tendency for most couples to resist change has constrained marriage. The Exceptional Marriage, on the other hand, is an organic, evolving process. Such a relationship is continually unfolding. It is a pathway to discovery. Or, as author and psychotherapist Judith Viorst (2003) puts it, "It also entails the brave, hard work of transforming these new, and sometimes shocking, perspectives into something expansive and creative, into an opportunity for a husband and a wife—and a marriage—to grow up."

Here, in a nutshell, is the answer to the question "Why marriage?" Through marriage we are called to become better human beings. This is marriage's most poignant purpose. Immersion into a shared life experience takes us beyond our limited, narrow, self-centered vision of existence. The creative potential of the committed relationship extends far beyond our own individual boundaries. Each one of us can surpass our most wildly conceived expectations when we allow another to participate in our unfolding as we participate in theirs. If you're looking for a transcendental experience, this is it!

Marriage is the primary environment in which to accept and appreciate diversity. It is the cornerstone of community. Without the ability to see the enormous value in living with someone so different, we can never really grow. Marriage is often bogged down by the efforts of both spouses to mold each other into their own images. One of the most significant reasons why couples end up in counseling is because they want each other to change into someone safe, familiar and predictable. But our emotional and spiritual maturity is directly linked to our ability to cultivate the diversity inherent in a vibrant marriage. We mature spiritually and affectively when we participate in each other's unfolding, wherever it takes us.

We become better people when we learn to feel more deeply. Our emotional life requires intimate communion with others. Not others as we wish them to be, but others who are free to be themselves. In our self–centeredness we hold ourselves at arm's length because we see difference as threatening.

Most of us learned in childhood that conformity made us feel safe. In marriage we tend to mutually encourage conformity, thereby squelching the vitality of diversity. In doing so, we dull our emotions and flatten our spiritual growth potential. Passion and growth are not based on how much we have in common or on having highly correlated compatibility profiles. They are the outgrowth of mystery and intrigue.

Can we let ourselves be amazed by our partners thinking, feeling, seeing, and acting differently that we do? What would happen if you gave up expending valuable energy on whether your partner picks up the towels, turns down the thermostat, eats too much sugar, fails to notice the changes you made in the in the living room, or leaves used dental floss in the sink? What would happen if you stopped trying to change your partner?

When we try to make each other conform to our model of perfection, we miss the potent possibilities imbedded in our differences. In marriage we have the opportunity to reach a sort of emotional enlightenment. Not a grandiose state of emotional bliss, but rather an ever-deepening capacity to feel. As emotional creatures, our light shines brighter and brighter as we develop our facility to hold and express our emotional truths. In our model, we call this "Full Self-Expression." The Exceptional Marriage cultivates this ideal. This is what we mean by going all the way.

What Do We Want?

We find comfort among those who agree with us, growth among those who don't.

—Frank A. Clark

When we decide to commit our lives to another human being, we do so for reasons that are less complex than we think. A mature relationship provides us with the opportunity to meet both our basic desires and our highest longings. It offers us both nurturance and challenge, comfort and provocation. That is an impressive and far-reaching opportunity. In this chapter we set the stage for a deeper exploration of going all the way in a long-term relationship by first identifying the motivating factors of life. In other words, what are we seeking? What propels us forward each and every day?

What we want in life can perhaps be summed up with three words: *protection*, *connection*, and *expression*. This trinity of desires guides and determines everything we do, think, and feel. It begins with our biological realities, extends right on through to our humanity, and goes all the way to our spiritual calling, which is to reach toward our greatest capabilities. We have our animal needs, our human desires, and our highest creative or spiritual yearnings. All are essential, all are fundamental to the exceptional marriage. Let's expound on each.

Protection

Every newborn wants to live. There are no suicidal infants. The call to life is strong, vibrant, and beautiful. The most compelling of all desires is to protect this precious life. It is instinctive. Every creature is wired to protect and secure its own existence. This desire to exist is the life-force articulating itself. We can refer to this desire as the self-preservation drive.

The vast majority of our waking attention is devoted to self-preservation. Biologically we focus on food, clothing, and shelter, and the accumulation of money as the means to preserve ourselves and our kin. We also work hard to preserve our psychological well-being and our growing sense of an autonomous self. In other words, I want to protect both my body as well as whoever it is I think I am.

Any threat to our survival (both body and sense-of-self) results in a biological call to arms. The autonomic nervous system kicks in and barks orders to flee, do battle, or seek a secure human connection. We'll return to the connection piece momentarily. The self-preservation drive compels us to protect and defend against any perceived threats.

The great irony of marriage is that our partners become our most formidable foes and our most powerful allies. The more somebody matters, the more threatening they can become. Most marital discord is the result of two people protecting themselves while in the throes of "fight or flight."

When Sarah tells Andre that she is fed up with his irresponsible spending habits, his fight-or-flight hormones surge, and he launches into a counterattack about her bitchiness that is purely a result of his self-preservation drive. He is threatened by her anger and responds in accordance with his biochemistry. She too responds to the rush of her own adrenaline supply. She then protects herself by using her most potent weapon—criticism. Back and forth they parry in an attempt to protect themselves from the dangers of love's cruel underbelly. Asking this couple to engage in "active listening" when they are both in full self-protection mode is to ignore biological imperative. During a perceived attack, empathy is a luxury they can ill afford.

We are motivated by the deepest urge to protect life, limb, and self-esteem. In our depths, we feel a primitive insecurity that is born out of the knowledge that our existence, biologically and psychologically, is fragile. In marriage, partners will look to each other for validation. In the deepest realms of commitment, it is our partners to whom we turn to help us feel whole, alive, and worthwhile. Autonomy percolates up from relationship. The great dilemma in our relationships is that we both fight with our partners in order to preserve our sense of self, and we need them to remind us who we are.

The drive toward self-preservation keeps us focused on stability and status quo. It is safety oriented. Any challenge to our stable identity evokes within us a fierce resistance. Put simply, our primal desire for self-preservation leaves us unwilling to change and grow. Relationships run into big trouble when self-protection dominates the landscape. To grow means to embrace the reality that a shared life requires being deeply affected by each other.

Connection

In our culture there is great homage paid to the god of autonomy. We are said to have achieved psychological health when we "individuate." It has become a self-help felony to behave "codependently." Yet to experience a solid sense of self is only part of the story. Human connection is predicated on the ability to feel our need for each other. Even as we discover the pleasure of our uniqueness and our autonomy, we look back over our shoulders to ensure we are not alone. As we bask in our egocentric glory, we lose sight of our longing for contact. In our modern world, as author and environmentalist Bill McKibben (2007) puts it, "We have a surplus of individualism and a deficit of companionship."

A child's desire for connection is at least as potent as his self-preservation drive. Studies show that the child's need for connection is so strong that he will literally place himself in harm's way to achieve it. For instance, a child will run toward and then past a frightening object or stranger in order to make contact with his mother. This early need for connection evolves into increasingly greater capacities for human engagement. Need is the bud that flowers into love. Paradoxically, the more autonomy we develop, the deeper our appreciation for each other is. Intimacy is the ever-increasing desire and ability to make real, undefended contact with another person.

In our personal and cultural urgency to establish our autonomy, it becomes so easy for us to pretend that we don't have needs. It is safer to live at a distance. So we create lives that allow us to turn away from each other. Many relationships hover in the space of mutually assured isolation. Partners create parallel universes and conjure the illusion of minimal need for each other. Couples may stay in touch by e-mail or cell phone, but not through belly laughs and emotional curiosity.

Let's be clear: Human beings need and long for contact. We never stop loving it; we just learn to disguise how important it is to us. We are sensual creatures. We are also emotional and spiritual creatures. Connection is critical to all these aspects of our humanness. Connection includes not simply touch but also the tenderness with which it is given. It means seeing and being seen, desiring and being desired, trusting, and laughing. It means the willingness to be in truth, and the willingness to let ourselves to be hurt.

Connection isn't all sweetness and light. It is much more real than that. Connection is wedded to conflict. When two humans negotiate their respective needs and wants, conflict will naturally arise. Too many relationships are dumbed down to a bland mutual coexistence by the avoidance of the intense feelings that genuine connection requires. We will return to the topic of conflict as an essential ingredient in Exceptional Marriages.

The only true experience of safety exists when we are in genuine connection with another person. While we fight for our autonomy, we can never fully let down our emotional armor until we establish human connection. From the newest newborn to the most ancient senior citizen, we are all quite desolate without connection. The essence of the word partner is part; we are a part of something larger. Through human connection, parts come together. The price of connection is the willingness to expose all of who we are—the good, the bad and the ugly. By shining a light on all of these aspects of ourselves, we realize that we are never as ugly as we imagine. Through the experience of connection, we enrich ourselves in ways that allow us to open up to our human potential.

Expression

By expression we mean that every one of us has a profound desire to bring out all of who we are and who we are capable of becoming. When we are focused on self-preservation, we essentially take a defensive posture toward life. Through connection, we let ourselves relax into the arms of another. To attempt connection feels risky; to have connection feels exquisitely safe.

We can call this most sacred of urges the full self-expression drive, or our "growth drive." It is expressed through impulses we have toward fulfilling our human potential and living an emotionally authentic life. The desire to comprehend oneself and the world, to experience pleasure, to find meaning, and to be creative are all aspects of individual self-expression. In relationships, this drive is characterized by the need for truth and emotional honesty, the desire to bring out the best in each other, the intention toward pleasure and mutual fulfillment, and the ultimate longing for love.

When we are motivated by the self-preservation drive, our attention is turned outward toward possible threats or obstacles to our survival or well-being. In most relationships, this means that partners are overly focused on what is happening with the other whenever there is conflict. Each is operating more from our ancient self-preservation "iguana" brain in an effort to prevent harm.

In self-expression, attention turns inward. Each partner is less concerned about what the other has done to them and more about what they themselves experience or feel. From self-expression, we tend to look at our own part in the conflict, and we are more motivated to understand and to make connection than to be safe or right. We operate more from the "higher" forebrain, where our full creative potential resides.

The drive toward self-preservation and the drive toward full self-expression together constitute our human motivation. Self-preserving motives are primarily egocentric and separating. Self-expressing motivations are more unifying or "spiritual." Both are critical to human adaptability. Connection is the bridge between the two. When we feel an attachment to another, we can relax the white-knuckle grip on self-protection and venture into the infinite space of our own creative aspirations.

The Exceptional Marriage places heavy emphasis on full self-expression. Such couples are perpetually challenging the status quo. Each partner wants more from life than paying the bills, watching The Weather Channel, eating, sleeping, and taking an occasional vacation. They are risk-takers, admirers of autonomy, and lovers of intimacy. These couples know that how they see themselves as individuals evolves as they continue to express their unique capacities. The relationship itself is an all-terrain vehicle for supporting full self-expression.

In self-expression, we ride the tide of our present experience. We engage with the world through our attunement to what is. We are not reacting so much as "co-acting" with life. In doing so, we learn, we grow, we evolve. Yet we miss out on all these possibilities when we get trapped in our past. We live in the past when we are trained to see every new situation through the lens of our personal myths.

Too Much Thinking

○ ○

These precious illusions in my head did not let me down when I was a kid./And parting with them is like parting with a childhood best friend.

—Alanis Morissette

We should take care not to make the intellect our god; it has, of course, powerful muscles, but no personality.

—Albert Einstein

In our work with couples, one thing stands out above all else: There is too much thinking going on. When we use our ability to think abstract, linguistic thoughts, we take one giant step away from experience. Let's say that Terry notices that Owen appears to be upset. She has a fear reaction in her body to this awareness but instantly turns to her thoughts instead. She tells herself that he must be angry because of something she did, and she frantically tries to figure out what it is. Instead of sitting in the experience, she develops a story about what she perceives. Whenever couples tell the story of why they have come to us for assistance, the profound discrepancy in their perspectives remains a source of wonder.

Story creates an illusion of safety and control. Our linguistic minds are noise machines that in part help us avoid emotions that we deem unacceptable. We strive to explain rather than experience. The story brings a sense of coherency to our freewheeling emotions. The tale we tell can easily be controlled; our feelings, not so easily. Often, even in therapy the story supplants the client's experience. This is done in an attempt to help us feel normal, rather than to simply help us feel.

For instance, Mark tells his therapist that he stopped having sex with Octavia because she put on weight. The therapist helps the couple to see the connection between Mark's sexual avoidance and the fact that his father used to humiliate his mother and openly blame her for their lack of sex. A valuable insight indeed, but nothing has really changed. Mark is never encouraged by the therapist to enter into the uncomfortable truth of how he actually feels when he is making love to Octavia. His judgment of Octavia's body was only the tip of an emotional iceberg.

Beneath his chilly surface, Mark was angry about her indifference, fearful of his own performance, hurt by her criticisms of him, and very remorseful for what he saw as his own shallowness. Additionally, he loved her and found it difficult to be both erotic and gentle at the same time. Only in expressing these very crucial emotional truths was he able to break through his sexual impasse.

In cognitive-behavioral therapy, we often hear how the mind creates cognitive distortions about what is happening. But in a very real sense, the term cognitive distortion is a redundancy. All thoughts are about our experience, they are not quite the experience itself. A certain distortion exists whenever we create a story to make sense of the world.

Since all of our stories are interpretations of experience, they possess an element of myth. They are designed to explain things that may be difficult to make sense of otherwise. While they play a vital role in helping us to achieve a certain level of understanding, just as this book might, our thoughts also crowd out our direct experience of each other. Direct experience is more felt than understood.

Connection, as we highlighted in the previous chapter, is one of the three grand human needs. As we develop our thinking minds we tend to experience less of a connection with others. Ideas outweigh emotions more and more as we grow up. Yet it is through our emotions that we make real connections. All the analyzing, all the reading, all the meditating and contemplating we do has precious little impact on our connection to each other. Connection is a resonance of energy that happens most fully through our emotions. It involves the surrender of our intellectual craving to justify and explain in favor of the mutual vibration of soul and sinew.

At best, sharing our thoughts creates "connection lite." We understand each other a bit better and we have a common frame of reference, but that's as good as it gets. We can detail and catalogue our issues and problems, but there they remain. More frequently, our thinking results in very restricted interpretations of our experiences and takes us further away from each other. As Ben Franklin aptly said, "The most exquisite folly is made of wisdom spun too fine."

Couples create many of their troubles through their thoughts about what is happening between them. But as we will see, it is not in changing our thoughts from negative to positive, or from distorted to clear, that a full connection occurs. For couples to claim their capacity for creative self-expression, each partner needs to drop beneath the veil of cognitive chatter into a more spontaneous interaction with the world.

In researcher Howard Gardner's study on multiple forms of intelligence (Quoted in Chilton Pearce 2002), he discovered that nearly all young children before age four tested at the genius level. By the time the children reached their twenties, the portion reaching the genius level on the tests plummeted to two percent. This shocking result, according to Gardner, was due to humans' internal "Voice of Judgment." Our minds inhibit our creativity.

Marcia and I believe that it is by connecting to our vital emotional energy that we transcend the Voice of Judgment, not by replacing it with a more effective voice. Relationship is more experience than thought, but thinking has drowned out our experience and left us feeling far too separate, no matter how much we "communicate."

Often, as cognitive behavioral theory informs us the story we concoct will trigger an emotional reaction. As an example, Carla responds angrily to Daniel when she catches him ogling a younger woman. She holds a myth that "all men eventually cheat," and this foments her hostility toward Daniel. Creating a connection begins not with correcting her distorted thinking but with opening her willingness to express how she feels. This involves not only her anger but all of what she feels—or what we refer to as full emotional self-expression. It is nearly impossible to correct a myth before the corresponding emotions are expressed.

In Carla's case, she had developed a myth of "the universal male cheat" because her father and grandfather had both done just that to her mother and grandmother. Consequently she pounces on Daniel using interrogation tactics. She tries to get him to confess to what she already believes to be true: He would rather be with another woman. Her anger at Daniel is, of course, her misplaced rage and hurt at the men in her family.

By having a venue where she can express these long-denied feelings and the insecurity grafted to them, Carla is better able to distinguish Daniel from her male forbears. She can begin to see him more clearly—that is, beyond her myth. "Story," after all, comes from the same linguistic root as "storage." We store our ideas about the world and draw upon them to make sense of our lives. But we are operating from our history (again, rooted in the same word as *story*) when we rely only on our ideas. We miss the vitality of the moment.

The study of the human mind has taught us that we have two primary sources of memory: implicit and explicit. Implicit memories are what we commonly refer to as "body memories." They are felt memories—sensations and emotions that we cannot attribute to any consciously recalled event. These body memories often lead to what seem to be overreactions in our marital relationships. This is one reason why it is important for couples to have freedom of emotional expression. It allows them to release the emotionally charged energy of these body memories.

Carla feels strong reactions of rage and revulsion coursing through her body when she sees Daniel eyeing the younger woman. These reactions were wired in long ago. Hoping to change her thinking without addressing these implicit body memories is like wishing upon a star.

Explicit memories are the stories, or "narratives," we develop beginning in the third year of life. These life narratives provide us with a sense of continuity and meaning. The great wonder of humanity is that as we develop self-awareness, we are able to endow meaning to our experiences. Human beings, unlike any other creature on the planet, are meaning-making animals.

In the development of our narratives, we draw certain conclusions about "the way life is." Our narratives are colored and flavored by the limits of our understanding. The best we can do is interpret events to give our lives a semblance of order, justice, and control. These interpretations are our myths.

Again, in Carla's case, she may have reacted earlier in life to her mother's distress and carried those feelings inside herself. She then developed an over-generalized myth that all men are cheats in order to guard against the strong emotions of hurt, disgust, and fear.

The myths that we created in childhood helped us to feel as if we had some modicum of control over our feelings, impulses, behaviors, and—perhaps most importantly—our environment. Yet the heavy price we pay for this presumed control is the sacrifice of spontaneity. As a child, this was seen as necessary for survival, yet as an adult, avoiding the direct contact with our undefended emotions runs counter to the development of an exceptional relationship. In the Exceptional Marriage, partners sometimes feel more fear than others in relationships because they are willing to challenge the myths and risk releasing the banished emotions.

In the remainder of this chapter, we will identify some of the more important characteristics of these myths so that we can appreciate how they impact our ability to go all the way in our exceptional relationships.

Myths are stories we create to protect us from the raw emotions we experience when our innocent self-expression is assailed.

Prior to the development of our myths, we confront head-on our unadulterated reactions to an unpredictable world. Myth, in essence, is our cognitive front line of defense. We diminish our own painful reactions to a world we have no control over by employing them.

For example, one man recently described how his mother was hospitalized for depression when he was four. This was a devastating experience for him. The myth he devised was that he was too much trouble for his mother, thus it was he who drove her to need hospitalization. This narrative allowed him to imagine that he had more control than he actually did. In intimate relationships, as an adult, he carries the myth that he is "too much" and that he will be abandoned if he expresses his need. As this man became more able to connect to his undefended feelings, he opened up to a deep pain, helplessness, and fear of loss. His myth served to protect him from the full force of his painful reality and to prevent him from experiencing again his original, anguished feelings.

Myths are over-generalizations that are often mixed with magical thinking.

Because the bulk of our myths develop in early life, the conclusions we draw are very simplistic and black and white. Our myths are typically sweeping conclusions that have no room for nuance. Additionally, children's minds have less capacity to distinguish fact from fantasy, so myths are often riddled with superstition and the belief that one can influence the outer world merely by thinking.

Ritual obsessions are clear examples of magical-thinking based myths. For instance, Jack Nicholson's character in the movie *As Good As It Gets* had to avoid stepping on cracks on the sidewalk. Presumably he held a myth of dire consequences if he deviated from his ritual.

Over-generalizations are the stuff of myth. These global conclusions we draw so limit our self-expression that we can never truly grow up. Standard over-generalizations include:

- "The world is dangerous."
- "Strong feelings are bad."
- "Mommy is perfect."
- "If I'm bad daddy will drink."
- "All girls are untrustworthy."
- "All boys are hurtful."
- "If I express need I will be disappointed."
- "If I'm not always on my guard, someone will take advantage of me."
- "Life is all about performance."
- "My impulses are evil."

Myths emphasize a certain aspect of the world and marginalize or diminish others.

What we mean when we say that myths result in marginalizing important information is that people tend to focus on all the data that reinforces the myth and tune out everything else. Let's say that Ethel has been dating Julius for three months. She is convinced that he is the most compassionate man on earth. She marginalizes those nagging instances when he tries to control her actions. She says, "He does it just because I am so important to him." When we marginalize such behaviors and our own genuine reactions to them, we set ourselves up to be used or abused. Julius conversely holds a myth that if he is not vigilant, Ethel will find somebody better. His mother had constantly teased him about his masculinity and compared him negatively to his brothers. As a result, he marginalizes all the ways that Ethel compliments him.

Myths lead to the development of habits, which narrows and conditions our behavior.

Habitual, ritualized styles of living are the universal tragic outcome of myth-based existence. So much of what we do is ruled by conditioned responses that we barely know that we are not free. Full self-expression is what awaits us on the far side of our habitual lifestyles. Habits include everything from how we dress to the way we say hello. While most habits appear to be benign, many of them constrict our spontaneity and access to pleasure. Habits can be outer behaviors or inner, patterned modes of thinking and feeling.

When we develop our myths, our feelings and behaviors will be calibrated by our history. Our interactions with our marriage partners become contaminated by habitual thinking. For example, Christine says that she really likes to be romanced. "I would love it if Raoul brought me flowers, but he never does." Raoul reacts strongly to Christine's request. He will not jump through hoops to please her—no way! It turns out that Raoul's mother was controlling and demanding of his father who, in turn, acted like a whipped puppy. Raoul's myth is, "If I am weak, then women will take advantage of me." So he equates Christine with his mom and is determined to never be like his dad. He habitually responds to Christine as if she were a "controlling bitch." His view of the present is historically contaminated.

Not surprisingly, Christine brings her own habits and historical contamination into the mix. While she thinks that she is simply asking for romance, her requests are disguised demands. She approaches Raoul not with a simple desire to be romanced, but with an implied ultimatum. "Bring me flowers, or I will be deeply disappointed in you and will criticize you unmercifully." Her myth is, "If I don't put pressure on him, he will never want to give to me freely." All her interactions with Raoul are contaminated by her history of feeling bitterly disappointed by men, especially her dad. It is Christine and Raoul's childhood interactions that form the habits that weaken their ability to express themselves fully.

Myths fall out of our normal awareness.

We are not consciously aware of our myths. They operate offstage, directing our everyday interactions. In order to grow, we need to bring our myths to consciousness. In our work mentoring couples, we first help each person identify the feelings that grow out of the myth. As another example, Marilyn said she couldn't trust Joe because he always had to put his needs first. They both worked and were raising a five-year-old son. She saw Joe as being like another child. Marilyn needs to have the opportunity to express the intense anger and mistrust she feels toward Joe before she can be open to seeing her myth. Indeed, as she eventually expressed and released these feelings, she suddenly realized that she wasn't reacting to Joe but to her stepfather. Out of this, she came to recognize her myth: "All men are selfish." She could then appreciate how she unconsciously marginalized all those aspects of Joe that did not square with her myth.

Myths are reflected in our physical structure and energy.

Our bodies react strongly when exposed to a world that doesn't always take kindly to our intense childhood expressions. As we incorporate myths to help us manage our own intense reactions, we develop what is called "body armoring." We can view armoring as the physical instrument of our emotional constriction. The myth reinforces the movement away from full emotional expression. The body then acts as if the myth is real.

Paul, for instance, tends to be exhausted frequently. He experiences his wife Joanne as very needy. His myth is that he cannot depend on others because they are too weak. As a result, his energy supply is often depleted and he tends to get sick. His body literally looks undernourished. Paul walks through life believing that he is on his own and that people either don't want to support him or are not capable of it. From this myth he lives a life deprived of adequate human support. His body, over the years, reflects that condition.

Overcoming a myth requires a willingness to surrender.

The process of personal growth involves a perpetual tension between resistance and surrender. For centuries, humanity resisted the notion that the earth revolved around the sun, and we still don't want to know that our personal myths are not real. At each developmental stage of life, we see the world from our limited vantage point. To the newborn, the concept of a "me" that is separate from "you" is as alien as politics to a lizard. The fourteen-year-old obsesses about a pimple, the twenty-five-year-old frets over getting the right job, the forty-three-year-old is concerned about the status of her 401(k), and the fifty-eight-year-old worries about Alzheimer's.

We all see the world through the lens of our limited experience. It is anxiety-provoking to open up to new possibilities. Surrendering means letting go of a small piece of one's preciously acquired autonomy. It means exposing ourselves to doubt. It is a fissure in our intellectual hubris. Or, as Thomas Szasz (1974) suggests, "Every act of conscious learning requires the willingness to suffer an injury to one's self-esteem."

The overindulgence in thinking actually takes us down the path of most resistance. There is pain and grieving involved in surrender. We resist it, sometimes to the bitter end. Changing our thoughts, our life narratives, requires an emotional transformation. To surrender is to open up to energy that is not entirely manageable. Letting go is a full-bodied experience.

Energy and Emotions

o o o o o o o o o o o o o o o o o o o o o o o o o
The end of the human race will be that it will eventually die of civilization.

—*Ralph Waldo Emerson*

The reason we are devoting a chapter to energy and emotions is quite simple: The transcendent goal of marriage is not to reach some state of peace and bliss; it's to feel more alive and to bring that aliveness to your partner and the world. This means bringing forth the full expressiveness of your emotional and creative self.

Every couple can be measured by their "energy quotient." A high energy quotient is characterized by more talk, more disputes, more laughter, more diverse activities, more touch, and a wider range of emotional expression. Low-energy couples are easy to spot by their predictability, over-investment in rationality, avoidance of conflict, aversion to all strong emotions, and increasing seriousness.

While there are many ways to define energy—electromagnetic impulses, life force, the divine spirit moving through us—we can all recognize its presence. We can look at depression as low energetic expression and mania as a highly charged, unchecked expression of energy.

In the human body, energy is expressed through sensation, movement, and the range of our emotions. As Christian de Quincey (2005) put it: "The body is an information processor; but it is much more than that. It is a meaning processor—it processes the constant stream of subliminal messages flowing into the body from the environment, integrating them with our felt experience, continually orienting us within the fields of matter, energy, and information swirling around us, so that we can distill a sense of direction and purpose."

In this chapter, we are going to highlight the role energy and, in particular, our emotions play in the marital relationship. We start with this premise: We human beings are governed much more by our emotions than we care to admit. While you will hear from all corners of the psychological universe that emotions need to be regulated, we believe that this mindset is antithetical to the development of the Exceptional Marriage.

Emotions are energy moving through us—e-*motion*. The regulation and management of this movement robs us of a portion of our humanity. Because of domestic violence concerns and a growing social discomfort with unhappiness in any form, we have seen a major shift toward a reliance on medications, reason, and behavioral techniques to conquer messy emotional "disturbances." While of course we need to do whatever it takes to vanquish all forms of domestic violence, in our view, we need more emotional freedom, not less. The tip-toeing around emotional expression results in relationships characterized by excessive use of prescription medications and employment of a wide range of tactics to avoid too much contact. In a sense, we have become a feeling-averse culture. Yet it is our emotions that infuse our relationships with life force. Our feelings are what give marriage its color, depth and flavor.

The Shared Energy Field

There is a road that goes from the eye to the heart that does not go through the intellect.

—G. K. Chesterton

The simplest way to describe energy is "movement." Whether it's the movement of our cars as we burn gasoline or the movement of our bodies as we burn calories, kinetic energy is the common denominator. For our purposes we will refer to kinetic energy, here as simply energy. Human energy is expressed as muscle movement, thoughts, and emotions. Every bit of energy we expend affects the world around us in some way. In this respect, all energy is shared; it's not something we can keep to ourselves. In groups of people, we may hear that "the air is heavy with excitement" or that "tension is so thick you can cut it with a knife." This is what we mean by shared energy.

Biochemist Dr. Mae Won Ho (Quoted in Chilton Pearce 2002) describes shared energy as such: "(E) ach of us has the waves of every other organism entangled within our own make-up … We are participants in the creation drama that is constantly unfolding. We are constantly co-creating and re-creating ourselves and other organisms in the universe, shaping our common futures, making our dreams come true, and realizing our potentials and ideals."

The exchange of energy that occurs between partners is so rapid and so abundant that it is virtually impossible to stay conscious of it all. There is one never-ending "passion play" of energy exchange we learn to regulate as a way of managing our interactions. This is the vibrant interchange of energy that we call the "shared energy field."

Let's say Ann comes home and is looking forward to seeing Henry. The moment she enters into his space, each of them fires off various emotional and energetic reactions. She may have an urge to kiss him but notices he's preoccupied. She thus holds off or offers a perfunctory smooch. Then she feels a wave of sadness or disappointment. Ann gives off both approach and avoidance energy toward Henry. He may see her and immediately feel a need for her to soothe his worries, but he also feels caution because he fears she won't be available. Simultaneously he feels attracted to her sexually. When she kisses him without enthusiasm, he experiences a tinge of hurt. As they continue to engage, they slip into "busy talk" and keep missing the juice of what is happening below their necks. All the little desires, needs, resentments, sexual urges, fears, and hostility, etc., go unnoticed.

This plethora of emotional interchange is the fuel that drives the Exceptional Marriage. Most couples miss the forest of emotional abundance in favor of a debate over a small piece of root rot. As de Quincey describes it: "Bodies in nature spoke to each other long before the development of grammatical speech ... Our only hope is to reinvigorate the language of the body ... to feel again the pulse of natural kinship."

In our mythology around autonomy, we have come to believe that our partner's moods should have no effect upon ours. If he's having a bad day, it should not affect her happiness; to do so is to be co-dependent. The reality is that we are profoundly affected by our partners. When we enter the same room, our bodies resonate in a symphony of energetic interactions. We can use our consciousness to make sense of some of what is going on between us, but there is no escape from the effects we have upon each other. The longer the duration of the relationship, the more chance we have of comprehending what is going on. His being upset will impact her emotionally, physically and cognitively. This does not mean that she is to blame for his distress, or that she has the power to alter it (though she can be a strong influence). It means that our shared energy field is alive and continually impacting both of us.

This reverberation of emotional energy casts fresh light on marital interaction. Feelings choreograph our connections far more than we imagine. Our emotions do not happen in isolation; they instigate each other, but not in a simple cause-and-effect manner. One's anger may in different circumstances spark another's fear, concern, guilt, reciprocal anger, or hurt. We can be angry at, with, or through another. To be angry through another person means one partner becomes the conduit for the other's withheld hostility. A wife, for instance, may constantly yell at her sullen and unresponsive husband. She becomes the carrier of anger for both of them and expresses his for him.

Who's Fault Is It?

As we'll see shortly, couples invariably drift into highly constricted and predictable modes of interaction, which effectively dull the senses to the waves of energetic exchanges perpetually commingling. The shared energy field between spouses is characterized by a swirl of subtle (and not so subtle) energy exchanges that result from each partner's experience in the moment, and is colored by all previous interactions—including the implicit body memories we talked about earlier.

We are continually reading and misreading, attuning, and distorting our feelings, thoughts, and behaviors as we commune with each other. There is no possible way we could be conscious of every energy interchange. It would be like trying to drink from a fire hose. In our attempt to hold some semblance of understanding, we learn to define what is happening between us using a cause-and-effect line of reasoning. When the richness of the shared energy field gets distilled down to simple cause-and-effect explanations, we can easily fall into cycles of blame exchange.

As intelligent creatures, we try to create security out of the chaos of unexpected and uncontrollable energies by developing, As Marcia and I described in the previous chapter, narratives and myths, which are our personal stories about what is happening. Our stories are translations from the language of energy to the vernacular of ideas. While our narratives are fundamental to our humanity, much gets lost in translation.

Let's look at a simple example. Newt and Olivia come to Marcia and me for mentoring. Olivia recounts her tale of marital woe. Newt, according to Olivia's narrative, is careless with money, obsessed with work, and he yells too much at their son Johnnie. Of course Newt has a much different narrative. Olivia, by his reckoning, has lost her sex drive, tries to control his every move, and is over-indulgent with Johnnie. By the time they enter the mentoring process, their narratives have hardened into concrete, immutable definitions of what is happening between them—a classic blame exchange.

This couple, like nearly every couple, defines the situation as one where "my partner is the cause and my reactions are the effect." By creating narratives in this way, partners make sense, at least in their own minds, of what they experience. But in doing so, they completely overlook the richness of the shared energy field that imbues marriage with its mystery and possibility. The personal narrative each partner concocts, while containing tidbits of truth, marginalizes the most important aspects of what is actually occurring between them.

Beware "Because"

The most crucial tenet of the shared energy field is that there is no first cause. The principle of "no first cause" challenges each partner's reactive victim mentality. All couples tend to think about what occurs between them as a simple cause-and-effect interaction. In the blame exchange it plays out as, "I am *this* way because you are *that* way." Each partner is tethered to the belief that they are merely reacting to the other's behavior.

Thus in Olivia's narrative, she tells us, "I'm not interested in sex when Newt gives more attention to his job than to us." But Newt will declare with equal conviction, "I've drifted away from Olivia because she's so damned focused on Johnnie and could care less about sex." Each description sounds plausible to its inventor, and indeed there is some truth to their narratives. Narratives, however, are grounded in linear thinking. Thoughts line up sequentially, while energy moves freely. Both of these descriptions of "the problem" marginalize the exquisite complexity of shared energy.

The more we sharpen our focus on a particular point of view, the hazier the larger reality becomes. Olivia has convinced herself that she is merely reacting to her husband's rejection of her in favor of work. What is overlooked is that her reactions to Newt's disappearances include hurt and a fear that he doesn't love her. Also, she's angry that he is not sensitive to her insecurities about her body image since she gave birth. She wants to punish him and knows that withholding sex will do the trick. She also loves him and feels regret that she blames him for how she reacts.

Meanwhile back at the ranch, Newt, too, holds back big chunks of his emotional truths in favor of his narrative, "Olivia, the doting mom and ice queen." He fails to be conscious of all that he is experiencing. He feels hurt and jealous of his son. He's been worried about money, which has caused him to feel less sexual himself and fearful of his genital performance. He is angry with his wife because he doesn't believe she appreciates his efforts, and he judges her for her spending habits. Additionally, he appreciates and admires how she raises their son Johnnie and has difficulty letting her know.

The shared energy field is a lush jungle of emotions, thoughts, and behaviors that have no beginning or end. It is easy to see why problem-solving approaches to couples' complaints are inadequate. The depth and breadth of what is occurring between couples is truly magnificent. The goal in our mentoring work with spouses is for them to express more and more of their authentic hurt, fear, anger, desire, remorse, appreciation, and love. Because each partner matters to the other, they constantly trigger strong reactions, which, over time, get further hidden behind their narratives and resulting facades. de Quincey writes, "Causes are not something the senses can detect. They are always something added by the mind to whatever we happen to see."

Negative Emotions Are Positive

Marcia and I have come to recognize that all couples develop what we refer to as "control patterns" that are created in order to keep the flow of emotional energy manageable and safe. In particular, couples learn to avoid what we call the three primary restorative emotions: anger, fear and hurt. Often these feeling states are considered negative. They are anything but. Let's explore them briefly before we return to control patterns.

We call these three feeling states *primary* because, once the infant reaches a level of awareness where she knows she is a separate self, the three emotions begin to take form. Like primary colors, other emotions are shades or combinations of the basic three. Emotions are biological states of arousal that are largely triggered by our interactions. All humans share these primary emotional states, which serve two main functions. First, they alert us that something is amiss. Fear alerts us to danger, anger motivates us to protect ourselves, and hurt allows us to mobilize a response to loss. Second, the expression of anger, fear, and hurt help us to restore ourselves to a state of well-being. By expressing these feelings, we reestablish inner harmony. When we learn to hold back the expression of these emotions, we create internal imbalance and stress.

Each of us learns to put a lid on our primary restorative feelings in childhood. To have a full-bodied cry, to give vent to our natural aggression, to let fear ripple through us, all become verboten. Most of us come to experience these raw feelings as being too intense, so we learn to clamp down on their expression. By doing so, however, we cheat ourselves of our very life force. We make it nearly impossible to fully engage our more expansive feelings of love, joy, gratitude, and need.

When we learn to bypass the restorative feelings, we live inside a mask of how we think we ought to be. Self-preservation reigns while self-expression withers. Once we learn to hide our primary restorative feelings, we begin to live in a "collapsed" state where energy is consumed by holding itself back. As Joseph Chilton Pearce (2002) puts it, "Because of its [the mask's] massively unnatural, arbitrary and illogical nature, it requires an equally massive energy to sustain it."

The world around us usually conspires to dampen the intensity of our primary emotions, and we carry this prohibition into our relationships. Control patterns are the result, which we develop and cultivate when the person we commit to becomes more and more important to us. The great paradox in marriage is this: The more important my partner becomes, the more I attempt to control the intensity of emotions. Why? Because the more you matter to me, the more I have at stake, and the more I stand to lose. As a result, the shared energy field gets cluttered with all sorts of actions and reactions designed to prevent exposure to the primary feelings and ultimately to our need.

Robert, for instance, constantly apologizes to Liz not because he believes he is wrong, but to avoid having to experience his anger and hurt at her criticisms. Liz forever nags Robert not because she is a control freak, but because she is fearful that he doesn't love her enough to want to care for her spontaneously. Neither wants to expose their raw primary feelings or the vulnerability of their need.

The establishment of control patterns generally results in one of two scenarios. First, couples become conflict-avoidant, which plays out over the long haul in what Marcia and I call an emotionally inhibited relationship. There is a pallor of resignation in these marriages, and such couples look elsewhere to feel alive. Second, are those relationships that generate a steady hum of bickering and blame. These couples are forever taking swipes at each other in subtle or more overt ways. While their energy is higher than conflict-avoidant couples, it rarely releases into other emotions. In both situations, couples are controlling the natural flow of emotional energy. We will return to control patterns in more detail in the next chapter.

Energy is in a continual state of either intensifying or releasing. This is referred to in the branch of body-oriented psychotherapy called Core Energetics as "charge and discharge." For instance, sexual arousal is experienced as energy-intensifying (charge). Orgasm is felt as an energetic release (discharge). Anger is charged energy, while crying is often a discharge. Exceptional couples readily enter into this natural flow of excitation (charge) and surrender (discharge). Intensifying energy tends to buttress our sense of autonomy, while releasing encourages intimacy. When we stop resisting this, we generate a higher energy quotient in our marriages. Many couples unfortunately tend to dwell in Middle Earth where they never get too excited nor do they allow themselves to fully surrender to the tender, vulnerable spaces of real intimacy. This surrender may be felt as authentic need, sadness, empathy, fear of loss, remorse, gratitude, or love. Control patterns keep us in Middle Earth where we simply don't allow ourselves to get too affected by our partner.

Conflict Engagement

This brings us to our final observation about energy. The free exchange of emotional energy in marriage will invariably result in conflict, or what marital therapist David Wile (1993) calls "nongenteel forms of fighting." The essential nature of conflict is to allow enough charge to build up that we can then surrender into intimacy. Therefore conflict is vital to an exceptional marriage. Until each one of us is charged up enough to feel our sense of self (autonomy), we can never fully surrender into intimate contact. Conflict permits us to feel *ourselves* before we feel our *partner*.

In our view, approaches to couples' work that emphasize "conflict resolution" skills are missing the true function of conflict. Good, healthy conflict has little to do with conversational etiquette. Its purpose is to charge up both spouses in a way that ultimately grants them access to tender, connecting feelings. In the Exceptional Marriage, fighting is the only realistic path to intimacy. Not the flaccid kind of fighting characterized by accusations, complaining, or self-pity. A good fight incorporates hate and love simultaneously. If we can't hate, we dilute the love.

Marcia and I recognize that hate is a potent four-letter word that evokes a strong, negative reaction in most people. But we need to appreciate what hate really is. Hate is the shadow cast by our vulnerability over the bright sunshine of our love. What we really hate is not our partner, but how much importance we have bestowed on our chosen one. Because they matter so damn much, we are deeply distressed by their character flaws and human foibles, as well as by how easily they can point out ours. Hate is incendiary hurt. "I hate you!" really means "I hate what you do to me!" Of course, rarely do we admit to such an intense reaction. Instead we will squelch our hatred by creating a narrative of our partners as stupid, irrelevant, hopeless, unattractive, critically flawed, or just not the right one. Good conflict allows us to build up and then surrender our resistance to feeling everything intimacy demands.

We cannot (and should not) try to put an end to conflict. Indeed, relationships are defined by conflict. It's only a relationship when one stands in relation to another. This means that we are different. Relationships are distinguished by differences, and differences invariably create conflict. If our differences don't bump up against each other, we become the same. Conflict is really a celebration of our differences—the acknowledging of relationship. Vive la conflict!

Control patterns emerge from the growing demand for sameness and predictability, and from the resistance to our primary feelings. Conflict is often the key to breaking the stranglehold of our control patterns. Unless we are willing to engage in conflict and place some stress on the control patterns, our interactions will become less robust and increasingly cautious. When couples opt for harmony over the dicey prospect of confrontation each partner loses a golden opportunity to evolve and learn from each other. Over the course of Drew and Nancy's fifteen-year marriage, for instance, she gradually gave up going out with her friends because he wanted her around all the time. Instead of confronting Drew with her frustration at his neediness, Nancy stayed home but acted cold and withdrawn. Drew was controlling against feeling his fear and insecurity and Nancy her anger and its consequences. This couple needed to learn how to have a good healthy fight to prevent the all too familiar "relationship drift" into apathy. Couples need conflict in order to stay engaged in each other's lives and to grow. If Nancy had challenged Drew, he may have had to take a closer look at where his insecurities came from.

Marcia and I prefer to emphasize "conflict engagement" rather than what is conventionally referred to as "conflict resolution." By this we mean that the emphasis should be on the experience of conflict rather than the outcome of conflict. Conflict resolution results in satisfying the content of any particular dispute. Engagement results in satisfying the need to deepen our heart connection. In conflict resolution, problems are solved; in conflict engagement, problems are dissolved. They melt away as we see the deeper truths that underlie them.

Basic Principles of Conflict

1. Most conflict is inherently good.

2. Conflict serves a biological function of allowing individuals to charge and discharge built up energy.

3. Conflict is part and parcel of mature interaction. Couples need to exert their influence on each other by expressing their differing ideas, values, intentions, or emotional reactions.

4. Good conflict is "improvisational." It does not follow a predetermined script and is often messy and scary before it leads to deeper connection.

5. Erotic energy is often embedded in conflict. When power greets power, sexuality flourishes.

6. Differences between spouses lead to stimulation, which then leads to growth.

7. Creative self-expression is dependent on conflict.

8. Honest conflict charges our energy and opens the way to more tender emotional expression.

9. Physical violence is not part of conflict. (It's actually conflict avoidance.)

10. Control-based conflicts are used to protect against our more vulnerable feelings. They never get beyond self-justifying and accusation.

11. Couples will remain in blaming conflict until each partner can admit to their desire to hurt the other. There is a revenge factor in many of our conflicts, and it needs to be acknowledged to be released.

12. Most conflict has little to do with issues and much more to do with finding intimacy through the pathway of autonomy. In other words, we need to first be able to speak up for ourselves before we can listen up to our partners.

13. Lack of honest conflict is the great destroyer of many marriages.

14. Conflict between spouses is often a reflection of each partner's internal conflicts.

15. Honest conflict typically leads to a deepening awareness of disowned aspects within oneself.

16. Good conflict often results in an "ah-ha" moment for one or both partners as they drop the veils of tightly held myths, or they drop into a restorative feeling.

The Four Stages Leading to the Exceptional Marriage.

o o o o o o o o o o o o o o o o o o o o o o o o o

Everything that is in the heavens, on the earth and under the earth is penetrated with connectedness, penetrated with relatedness.

—Hildegard of Bingen

Have you thought what it costs to be normal?

—James Hillman

In this chapter, we lay out the four stages that lead to the Exceptional Marriage. Long-term relationships go through an "evolutionary" or developmental process. By this Marcia and I mean that the committed relationship must be open to change and discovery in order to thrive. The idea here is simple. The moment we conclude we know our partners, we stop evolving. There is always and forever more of ourselves to be expressed.

By defining the course of marriage as a developmental process, our desire is to "de-pathologize" the problems that inevitably occur as two people forge a life together. Most problems in marriage spring not from dysfunction but from an inability to express what is going on in our hearts and spirits. The development of a relationship involves never-ending revelations. We reveal more and more as we come to know ourselves on ever-deepening levels. Our character develops through exposure to life's drama. The birth of a child, a miscarriage, a new job, the divorce of a close friend, a spouse's success, an affair: each offers an opportunity to discover something new.

Marriages do not start out as exceptional. Nearly anyone can get married. To go all the way, couples typically traverse through these four primary stages:

1. The Eros Stage

2. The Control Stage

3. The Transition Stage

4. The Exceptional Marriage

Attaining an Exceptional Marriage takes many years of effort and devotion to the process of developing a deep intimacy. While there are no easy shortcuts, it is possible to optimize the chances of success by knowing what to look for. As the saying goes, "If you don't know where you're going, you won't know when you get there." So let's take a closer look at each of these four stages.

1. The Eros Stage

> *When I am with you, we stay up all night. When you are not here, I can't sleep. Praise God for these two insomnias! And the difference between them.*
>
> *—Rumi*

Most couples who marry first go through the magical, synapse-burning, "everything is right with the world" stage of infatuation. The drama and fanfare that trumpets the arrival of newfound love is incomparable to any other of life's many offerings. Eros appears on the scene in flamboyant style as we are suddenly and insatiably consumed with every nuance of our new lover's thoughts, actions, and feelings.

Marcia and I call this the Eros Stage because the energy that exists between new lovers is intensely erotic. Our definition of erotic encompasses more than the conventional idea of potent sexual feelings. Eros refers to the great charge of passion that is ignited when two people hit it off. This passion, while certainly sexual, also allows individuals to shed their defenses and exhibit the best of who they are. It is an insurgency of the heart that is fueled by an injection of neurohormones. In particular, Eros is ignited by a flood of dopamine into the bloodstream. This hormone, along with another called norepinephrine, serves to throw us into a high state of emotional exhilaration that can leave us so consumed that we'll sacrifice all else to be with our lover. Eros is unchained romantic love combined with a liberal dose of lust. We are hormonally intoxicated when in its throes.

Eros is the source of creativity, wonder, and heart. It is a mythic force that elicits our longing to discover each other. While in its grip, we take great pleasure in uncovering the mysteries of our partner. Couples believe they are "madly in love" at this juncture. But what they really are is "madly in Eros." They can't stop thinking about each other. Founder of Core Energetics John Pierrakos, MD (1987) writes, "Eros is a unique experience but it is not love itself.... People under the spell of Eros are radiant—their eyes shine, their skin glows, their bodies exude power and joy.... Eros is also the foundation upon which two people can build an edifice of love. But creating this abode requires a great deal of hard work."

The gift of the Eros Stage is that it alters our consciousness and allows us to move beyond survival mode, if only temporarily. It is a transformative energy that gives us the impetus to reach our highest potentials. For a brief period, we feel a connection to another human being and to life itself in a way that transcends all insecurities, all differences. Pierrakos continues: "Eros strikes with such a powerful impact that it breaches the most rigid defenses. Suddenly, without warning, it shakes up your defenses; it brings movement, life, hope....

Eros transforms us from weak to powerful, hard to soft, rigid to flexible."

Eros gives us a peek into what is possible. In its embrace, we see beyond all the insecurities and habits we cling to so tightly. But Eros will soon subside. In fact, by the time people actually marry, it will have waxed and waned. Frequently, Eros is not the determining factor in the decision to wed. Thoughts of marriage often emerge *after* the Eros Stage dissipates.

Sometimes people are looking to reinvigorate Eros by getting married. When both spouses are absorbed in Eros there is a degree of heightened self-expression. Partners feel more creative and wildly alive, but there is little willingness to confront the sore spots. Primary feelings are avoided and literally overwhelmed by the joy of erotic immersion. This is an unsustainable energy, so it won't be long before couples settle into their personal coterie of control patterns.

Eros abounds when people first connect, but it does not simply end six months into the relationship. While it will never again dominate the marital landscape as it once did, couples that continue to grow together find Eros popping up in a variety of ways. For example, sixteen years into their marriage, Ellie began writing poetry. Frank was deeply moved and inspired by Ellie's poems. He saw her in a new light.

Thus, while we describe Eros as dominant in the first stage, we want to emphasize that the path to the Exceptional Marriage is lined with numerous opportunities to feel the erotic power of this first stage. Once we conclude that we pretty much know our partners, Eros evaporates. Only when we appreciate the infinite mystery within our spouses do we keep it alive.

This initial stage of the Exceptional Marriage must, of necessity, give way to subsequent stages. As partners begin to entertain the possibility of long-term commitment, the world of love takes a few twists and turns. A funny thing happens on the way to commitment. As Eros retreats, a cozy coexistence emerges in its wake, which means both good news and bad news for most couples.

2. The Control Stage

> *We spend our time searching for security and hate it when we get it.*
>
> —John Steinbeck

If Eros ushers us into a romantic connection with a partner, it is the capacity to bond that sustains the connection. In bonding, couples melt into the warm and cozy embrace of familiarity and contentment. During this period, a truly amazing biological drama unfolds. The secretion of the neurohormones dopamine and norepinephrine begin to wane, only to be replaced by another wonder hormone, oxytocin. This is the same hormone that is used to induce labor in women. It is associated with a sense of contentment. Under the spell of oxytocin, couples bond.

This urge to converge, however, has its pitfalls. As partners become more familiar and coziness eclipses Eros, a flat patina blankets the luminescence of stage one. The quest for security hijacks the erotic spirit of adventure. Bonding becomes binding when relationships stop growing. Couples silently slip into survival consciousness as safety and harmony become more important than exploration and the possibility of enchantment. Bonding is a primitive form of connection that emphasizes safety over discovery. This is how it must be—safety first. Secure attachment to one's partner is primary, but it is not the ultimate purpose of long-term commitment.

Couples in stage two feel a certain comfort in their shared life, but also begin to dull their senses to each other. Indeed, we begin to construct images of each other that allow us to feel safe. So, for instance, Thomas may spend a lot of time joking about Geri's poor grasp of the English language, but fail to notice her incredible capacity to communicate from the heart. It is safer for Thomas to emphasize Geri's less developed aspects than to experience how great she truly is. To do the latter would leave him feeling a little less secure, a shade less in control.

One of the downsides of stage two is that we begin to try and mold each other in ways that allow us to perpetuate a seemingly safe and predictable marriage. It is not a coincidence that long-term relationships are often described as "enduring." It's sad to believe that endurance has become the standard of the healthy relationship.

In durable relationships, Eros doesn't simply die, it migrates. Whereas in stage one partners brought erotic juiciness to each other, eventually it pops up in all sorts of venues: playfulness and creativity with the kids; careers; sports; artistic endeavors; Internet porn; reading self-help books; and anywhere else but toward each other. Eros is a life force, and it will not be denied. But in stage two, spouses go into erotic lockdown with each other.

Couples often cross the connubial threshold already in control stage. Without realizing it, most married partners begin to hold back their life force in a monumental effort to avoid feeling the unwanted primary emotions. After opening so widely in Eros, couples tend to fall into repetitive and mutually reinforcing styles of interaction, or what author Daniel Siegel (1999) calls "interlocking states." These ritualized patterns of interacting are the offspring of our personal myths.

To give just one example, if a newlywed holds a myth that it is his job to act as his partner's savior in order to be loved, he will need his wife to be the damsel. In the Eros Stage, our hero will project an image (unsustainable in the long run) of absolute support. He will promise to make her life carefree. But in the Control Stage, this myth begins to exact a price, because buried inside every myth is a hidden demand. In the case of Mr. Savior, the concealed mandate is, "I'll be your strength, but you must never threaten me with your own strength." In the Control Stage, this myth is typically greeted by Ms. Damsel's mirror myth: "I must play weak in order to get the man to want me."

So, what exactly are we controlling in the Control Stage? The answer is simple: emotions. As we mentioned in the previous chapter, all couples develop unconscious patterns of interacting that are designed to prevent the expression of the primary restorative feelings of anger, fear, and hurt. These feelings are themselves responses to our basic human need for connection. When this need is threatened, the primary feelings will naturally erupt. But because they are experienced as so volatile, we come to believe we must tame them. So our interaction styles become tightly choreographed, and we build our dream home on the shores of Lake Placid.

As mentioned in the previous chapter, all couples in the Control Stage engage in one of two tactics. First, they collude to avoid conflict, which causes the relationship to flatline from terminal apathy. Second, they seek to place blame on each other for the loss of the erotic ideal that captivated them not so long ago. In both situations, the partners are evading direct contact with primary feelings.

In conflict avoidance, partners are essentially saying, "Let's not mess up our tidy images of ourselves by pointing out the truth of our limitations. Don't challenge me, and I won't challenge you." Harmony over truth is the silent choice. Here, couples are mutually afraid of rocking the boat. Couples in stage two think in terms of keeping the relationship stable above all else. The idea that change will occur is not one easily entertained by Control Stage couples. According to Siegel, "Interlocking states ... create a rigidity that prevents the partners from joining together ... At one extreme these ruts can be experienced as a sense of malaise or deadness, which each member of the pair may feel but be unable to articulate; at the other extreme, these ruts may be filled with anxiety and a sense of intrusiveness and uncertainty."

Conflict-avoidant couples will either eventually drift apart, each turning elsewhere to once again indulge in the thrill of Eros, or they will plod along in uneasy peace. These relationships lack the passion, vitality, and sense of expansiveness that epitomizes the Exceptional Marriage.

One such conflict-avoidant couple is Priscilla and Nick. Priscilla operates with a myth that says, "If I'm not highly sexual, you won't want to be with me." So she and Nick have sex five or more times a week. Nick holds the myth, "A real man should always want sex." Because they are conflict avoidant, they continue to have sex even when they may not want it, each for a different reason. Neither is willing to acknowledge the truth. When the inevitable day comes where Nick cannot perform, he will feel like a failure, and she will be threatened by the idea that he doesn't want her anymore. Frequent sex, in this instance, is a control pattern. Conflict avoidance is really myth-busting avoidance. Nobody wants their myths challenged because they do not see them as myths.

The need to insert blame into the equation also defines the Control Stage marriage. Second stage couples Marcia and I have worked with routinely have mastered the fine art of mutual blame. Conflict in these relationships habitually takes the form of "I'm right, and you're wrong," in all that argument's variations. Each person sincerely believes that "I am this way because you are that way." In their relationship Charlie swears he wouldn't lose his temper if Ray would just stop complaining about everything he does. With absolute equal conviction, Ray believes if Charlie weren't so defensive and resentful about his responsibilities, he would not have to confront him.

Blame germinates in self-preservation mode. Whenever we feel a threat to our sense of self, we are apt to employ blame as a first responder. Charlie's temper is like an old friend to him. From his perspective, if he gives it up, he is allowing himself to be controlled by Ray. He places himself in the false dichotomy of having to choose autonomy or relationship. In reality, we are not in an either/or battle, but rather a "both or neither" crossroads. Partners blame each other when autonomy feels threatened, but as we have said, there is no autonomy without connection.

Blame is enlisted in service of preserving our tenuous, myth-infused sense of self. Every spousal reproach chips away at our own delicately spun life narrative. Our spouses are very adept at ruining our convenient truths. They readily point out the inconsistencies in our stories. So we most often respond with reciprocal blame. Our personal myths are shaken because there is invariably a hurt-seeking missile of truth fired at us in every blaming statement.

To go back to our example couple, Ray tells Charlie he is insensitive. Charlie feels threatened by this because Ray's description embodies a tidbit of truth. He can be insensitive and arrogant, but this doesn't fit with Charlie's myth that he is only protecting himself from being controlled. So he blames Ray in order to preserve his illusion.

Blame cultivates resistance to change. Whenever we focus on assigning blame, it is an escape from self-discovery and an avoidance of self-responsibility. When partners engage in mutual blame, which is common in the Control Stage, they are ensuring stagnation. It is nothing short of amazing to see how astute each spouse is in describing the other's issues, problems, hang-ups, and shortcomings and how blinded each is to his or her own.

As long as partners are more concerned with what needs to change in the other rather than within themselves, the relationship will float on the surface of its potential. The potential in any relationship is wedded to each partner's readiness to reveal all that lies beneath the surface of blame. We only surrender the addiction to blame when we are willing to experience and express our raw primary feelings. Trying to get our partners to change via criticism and judgment will always and forever be met with resistance.

In stage two, couples cling tightly to the familiar. It goes against our human nature to change in response to our partner's judgment of us or even to our own self-judgments. Change only occurs in an environment of love, and love exists only when we can express all of who we are. Control patterns are anti-change behaviors that result in the inability to fully allow love to flourish. They are a contrivance of emotional manageability.

Each of us comes into marriage with our own unique array of quirks, oddities, and exasperating habits that arise from our genes, our wounds, and the intricate styles of hiding from our emotional truths we learn along the way. The Control Stage is characterized by the tightly woven patterns of interaction that serve to keep us from accepting the truth of who we really are. The control patterns Marcia and I have witnessed typically fall into one of two categories that are aligned with either avoidance or blame. We can refer to these as passive and aggressive control patterns. While there are countless possibilities, here are a few examples:

Passive Patterns

- Giving in order to get: using false generosity as a way to keep partner placid.

- Withdrawal, or literally avoiding one's partner

- Withholding: being unwilling to express your emotional fullness, both positive and negative, and particularly your need for connection

- Indecision and ambivalence

- Distraction

- Humor, smiling, false optimism

- Acting weak or wounded

- Trying harder to please

- Preemptive actions: doing or saying something as a way to circumvent a spouse's negative reaction (such as by getting off the computer when you hear your spouse enter the house)

- Self-flagellation

- Feigned concern or worry

- Using illness, exhaustion, injury, etc., to avoid intimacy

- Using spirituality to control against negativity

Active Patterns

- Using reason to convince partner

- Overwhelming spouse with strong non-primary feelings (jealousy, blaming anger, insecurity, etc.)

- Chronic demands for reassurance

- Threats of leaving

- Using sex as a way to avoid conflict

- Undermining partner's self-esteem

- Crying in order to manipulate the partner

- Affairs

- Bullying and intimidating

- Focusing on partner's limitations in order to avoid feeling how important she or he is

- Physical abuse

Another telltale sign of the control-based relationship is seen in the expression of need. Marcia and I see need as being expressed in two ways. First is what we can describe as the unmet needs from childhood. Suppose, for instance, a child's father dies when she is five. She may experience a "need" later in life to always know her husband's whereabouts. Thus the need is a holdover from childhood. Though it is experienced as a real need, knowing as an adult where her husband is at all times does not solve anything. It is a feeble attempt to take control of the uncontrollable. If "dutiful husband" chooses to pacify his wife's unmet childhood need, he will soon become "beleaguered husband" and she will still not feel safe enough.

Childhood needs can be detected by their urgency. "I need you to send me flowers" expresses a silent ultimatum. The energy behind the expression of childhood needs is intense and puts unfair pressure on a spouse to come through or else! Thus childhood needs are really indirect demands. Listen carefully to control stage couples, and you will hear the silent "or else" at the end of every request coming from childhood need.

- I need you to leave me alone (or else I will withdraw even more)
- I need you to be more romantic (or else I'll withhold sex)
- I need you to get a better job (or else I will humiliate you)
- I need you to make me feel safe (or else I'll punish you)

The true "or else" is, in actuality, more about the person expressing the childhood need. In essence that person is saying, "If you don't meet my childhood need, I will be confronted with feeling something I desperately don't want to feel."

Thus:

- I need to be left alone (or else I might expose my rage)
- I need you to be more romantic (or else I will have to confront my own sexual ambivalence)
- I need you to get a better job (or else I might have to face my own fears of insecurity or inadequacy)
- I need to feel safe with you (or else I'll have to confront my terror)

Childhood needs are a very real form of control each partner exerts upon the other in order to avoid leftover, unfinished emotional expressions from childhood. It comes down to this: "You have to protect me from facing feelings that I learned long ago are dangerous. It's your job to act precisely as I need you to in order for me to avoid uncomfortable emotions that I don't believe I could handle."

By and large, these childhood needs go unexpressed because we know on a gut level that they cannot be met by our partners. We also are ashamed of them. As one spouse described it, "I sometimes feel like I am this black hole of need."

In contrast to these childhood needs are our mature needs, which will be discussed in greater detail later. Mature needs are based in present-day, adult requirements for human connection. Predictably, as much as Control Stage relationships are keen to express childhood needs, they are loathe to reveal genuine need. While the phrase "I need you to ..." forecasts the coming of an childhood need, the straightforward "I need you" is the signature statement of a mature need.

Childhood needs are all about wanting something from the other. Mature needs make a statement about ourselves with no implied demand that the other provide something. Childhood needs originate out of the deficiencies of childhood. Mature needs come from our responsible adult selves. Most stage two couples do not allow themselves to fully feel the joy that comes with just needing each other's presence.

The majority of couples drift along in Control Stage for the duration of the marriage. Here is where couples begin settling for "as good as it gets." What they put in is what they get out. Little children who have not yet developed the consciousness to interact engage in what is called "parallel play." They sit side by side, each focused on their own entertainment. Similarly, Control Stage couples often engage in "parallel existence," with limited quality interaction. Not because they don't have the conscious capacity, but because they tend to hunker down into individual, habitual routines. The amount of time spent in actual interaction is distressingly meager. They may watch TV together, or even engage in family activities, but even here interaction can be parallel. They are separate together.

Such couples may display mutual respect, but they lack passion. Their conversations are short on emotional depth, and there is a noticeable dearth of healthy conflict. Instead there will often be a heavy dose of bickering or tepid civility. Additionally, stage two couples may talk behind each other's backs, or conversely, they may cover up their nagging negativity by idealizing their spouse. There may be a pre-occupation with security issues ("Our lives are so busy we don't have time for each other") and avoidance of confronting sexual dissatisfaction ("Our sex life is fine").

When couples dwell in the land of survival consciousness too long, they begin to accumulate a cache of secrets, or "withholds." These usually will not spill out until stage three. Most Control Stage couples don't say all there is to say about their sexual desires, fears, escapades, or hang-ups. They may avoid revealing shameful parts of their histories. They almost never express selfish and cruel feelings from their "lower selves."

These couples also tend to express guilt rather than genuine remorse. (The difference being that guilt is feeling bad about myself, while remorse is feeling bad about what effect I had on you.) Guilt is often expressed to get you to stop disliking me (control), while remorse is an authentic expression of empathy. My remorse invites you to feel, but guilt takes the focus off you and brings it back to me, thereby disallowing you your pain.

Fights in stage two will be reactionary and are almost never about what really matters. In fact, the fights are universally about defending and preserving one's autonomy. Another example: Reggie and Merrill fought constantly about child-rearing. Merrill thought Reggie was too lenient, while he believed she was over-the-top strict. They argued in great detail about nearly every decision. Many of these arguments took place in front of their two-year-old, Jamal. When this was pointed out to them, it created a leap of perspective as they saw that they weren't as concerned about Jamal's welfare as their arguments would suggest. This was an autonomy war and a self-righteous power struggle.

There is often a great deal of hidden competitiveness in the Control Stage. Each partner is threatened, often outside of his or her awareness, by the other's becoming too strong in the relationship. Consequently, there are indirect (or not so indirect) ways that each puts the other down. Sometimes it may appear good-natured, but there is a concealed need to diminish each other. This is the domain of the unacknowledged lower self—secret, toxic pleasure in our partner's failings. It's too shameful to admit, yet very real. In their marriage, Maureen constantly pokes fun at Artie's forgetfulness. Artie never misses an opportunity to point out Maureen's inability to balance the checkbook. Neither particularly enjoys the jabs. The couched competitiveness in this marriage leaves both Artie and Maureen weaker and more defensive. The emphasis on each other's faults creates an aura of caution and uncertainty.

As we have learned, the essence of control patterns is the mutual effort to inhibit the connection to and expression of primary emotions and mature need. Additionally, couples employ control patterns to avoid the intensity of deep, loving feelings. Marcia and I refer to this as a "contraction from intimacy." This plays out as an energetic collusion where one partner feels madly in love, but the other becomes reserved in response. It is as if it becomes intolerable for both partners to be wide open to each other simultaneously. The relationship can't seem to bear that much excitation or intensity.

Yet another indicator of Control Stage is what we call "commitment inhibition." What we mean here is that couples may make the outer vow of commitment, but emotionally and energetically, there is a tentativeness, a holding back, a "not quite ready to take the full plunge" consciousness. Couples may believe they are fully committed, but commitment is an evolutionary unfolding. In stage two, there is a vague fear, often unarticulated, that our partner may bail out if the going gets too rough. Equally, we are not fully sure of our own willingness to stay with this person. A little soul searching may lead a partner to the conclusion that he is staying more because of the complexity involved in leaving than because of a desire to be with his spouse. Indeed, the hallmark of the movement into the Transitional Stage is the confrontation of this commitment inhibition.

3. Transition Stage

> *Thank you for breaking my heart. Thank you for tearing me apart. Now, I've a strong, strong heart. Thank you for breaking my heart.*
>
> —*Sinead O'Conner*

The deconstruction of the controlled and calculated relationship begins here. The third stage leading to the Exceptional Marriage is a tumultuous one. The integrity of the existing relationship is seriously challenged during this time. Couples in stage three often question whether they are with the right person or whether they are cut out for marriage. This is a powerful, frightening, and yet promising time for couples.

It is our experience that couples who are unwilling to enter the crisis of the Transition Stage can never achieve the Exceptional Marriage. When confronted with the terrifying prospect of overhauling what they have held dear, they often retreat back to the pseudo-security of the Control Stage. Blame-based couples will often enter marriage counseling in the Control Stage in an attempt to employ the therapist to help fix the other. Conflict-avoidant couples usually only seek counseling if they break out of the Control Stage into the Transition Stage.

While stage two is characterized by preserving what we have, the Transition Stage evinces a calling for change. As a couple enters into transition, the lethargy of survival is supplanted by the electric charge of uncertainty and possibility. Couples who have been married for fifteen or twenty years suddenly are asking themselves whether what they have is what they want. To this we say hallelujah! While we certainly do not wish for people to suffer, there is a necessary angst that is part of the dues we must pay to go all the way. Running and hiding from this beast will crush our spirits and eviscerate our power. Growing up demands that we take a good hard look at what we have created and be willing to admit that it just isn't enough.

We call this the Transition Stage because it is defined by breaking through the mold of familiar habits, patterns, and styles of interaction. Or it signals the end of the marriage. A fair number of couples who hit stage three will divorce. Sometimes this is the right decision, but often it only means that each partner was unwilling to confront the myths and the primary, powerful emotions that reside beneath. We have seen long-term relationships among our own friends that perished under the weight of having to look deeper. Sadly, the most golden opportunity that life may ever offer them is tossed into the waste bin of self-preservation consciousness.

Saying good-bye may not mean physically leaving; it may mean letting go of controls and embracing authenticity. This can be an agonizing birth. Confronting what is missing means having to change—never an easy path. Transition Stage couples feel their whole infrastructure lurching toward collapse. This is as tough as it gets. Because they don't know where it will lead, it takes great courage to acknowledge that something is amiss. Transition is the moment of reckoning.

Sometimes it is heralded by an "out of the blue" sexual affair. This is not the kind of affair that a Control Stage spouse might engage in. In the Control Stage, affairs are laden with a quality of avoidance. They occur as a way not to deal with emptiness. In Transition, the affair is an incendiary device used to wake up the somnolent spouse. This affair says, "You see, I still have mystery about me. Do you care?" While not something to be endorsed, the Transition Stage affair often creates something positive. If you listen carefully, the spouse having the affair is usually saying, "I want more of this from our marriage" rather than "I want out."

As couples traipse along through the Control Stage, sexuality, too, falls into predictable patterns. Partly this occurs because spouses begin to take on the identity of "family." Especially if children arrive, sex partners gradually morph into Mom and Dad. They take on a familial energy with each other. Sex loses its mysticism and passion. After all, who wants to have sex with family?

In stage three, the comfort of the familial relationship becomes stifling. Partners want more eroticism. If they possess the courage, they may begin to express their sexual dissatisfactions with each other. "Painful" may be an understatement as one partner reveals to the other long held disappointments. It is hard to hear that your spouse may have not liked certain aspects of your lovemaking. It is at least as difficult to say what you have been unhappy with. This disclosure may break the rules of positive communication, but we believe the expression of withheld disappointments can free up the logjam of sexual energy.

Transition energy is rife with discomfort. This is not the time to talk by the rules. It is a "no holds barred" period where each partner may threaten the other with displays of serious doubt. Not the bogus doubt of Control Stage, where misgiving is utilized more as a bludgeon, but the bona fide concern of one who genuinely questions the future. Transition is experienced as crisis, and it is just that.

The crisis of Transition Stage is the roiling uncertainty of the future. All those years together might go up in smoke. Couples must be willing to challenge the embedded comfort of the Control Stage and expose themselves to higher levels of emotional intensity. This requires entering into the abyss of uncertainty. It means giving up the false hope that things will just work out. In Transition, couples must confront hopelessness. While we have been schooled to believe that loss of hope is psychologically unhealthy, it can be the catalyst for great new beginnings.

Take, for instance, Roberta. She refused to give up hope that her gambling-addicted husband Lyle would get his act together. She survived on hope over eighteen years of crushing losses. One clear day, she emerged from being buried in this "toxic" hope and admitted to herself that Lyle was not going to change. The present situation was, she recognized, beyond hope. Was it a coincidence that her leaving was followed by Lyle's epiphany that he had a problem?

Sometimes hopelessness does not result in story book endings, but always it signals the recognition of some long-denied truth. The hope that violence, infidelity, emotional emptiness, sexual boredom, or blaming dialogue will simply go away one day is antithetical to growth. Transition couples crash into the abyss of hopelessness that life cannot continue as it has. This awareness creates a demand for something greater. It is time to step up and find one's self-expression or to go back into self-preservation hiding. The control-based couple is characterized by the old adage, "They died at forty and were buried at eighty." The transition couple insists on rebirth.

Conflict during the Transition Stage evolves from the "I'm right, you're wrong" variety and begins to embody other elements. Here, couples are more able to acknowledge lower-self negativity. In marriage mentoring, we often see that couples are now willing to express their hidden competitiveness, cruelty, selfishness, and hostile fantasies. For these to emerge in a structured way frees up the depressed energy between them. Couples absolutely need to reveal the hidden hostilities and negativities that are part of the human condition.

In a mentoring session, we encouraged Mara to expose her cruelty to Lance. When she was able to reveal how she hated when he would go into his shell, we invited her to express more. She opened up to how she secretly wants to humiliate him and make him feel like a failure. In mentoring, we give couples free reign to express all this with passion. As Lance heard Mara's lower-self feelings, he reacted primarily with relief. While her words were hurtful, he already knew this about her by the way she treated him. Having it out in the light of day allowed him to breath easier. In turn, he felt safer expressing his lower-self reactions toward her. He revealed how a part of him enjoyed making her feel insecure about her body.

Opening up to these "darker" places we all possess distresses the Control Stage edifice. Couples actually become more alive. Yet until they reach the Transition Stage, they are not ready to take ownership of these sensitive truths. Passion is rekindled when we are able to challenge our own and each other's myths. Couples in transition want more passion, and the only way to get it is by moving past the limited options of being nice, blaming, or frigid. Once partners can acknowledge their shadowy negativities, full self-expression becomes a possibility. Just knowing that we can hurt each other has the paradoxical effect of making us aware how much our partners matter.

In marriage, the feelings of the destructive lower self must be confronted before people can truly become intimate. Any attempts to circumvent the lower self results in a neutered interaction. All of us carry the simple negative emotions that are part of humanity. We also hold the even darker feeling of cruelty or the desire to cause harm that results from the avoidance of our full self-expression. We conceal much of our inner life, and as a result, we harbor negative intentions toward others. In the Exceptional Marriage, we embrace this reality. Truly exceptional couples learn how to reveal their darkest and most vulnerable truths to each other

As we release lower-self expression, we begin to engage in healthy conflict that will arise when two strong, mature people hold opposing opinions, beliefs, or preferences. Such conflict is reflective of two individuals who are unwilling to either give up themselves or the relationship. Transition relationships begin to lead into the Exceptional Marriage when couples realize that the marriage is their best opportunity to evolve as humans and explore the upper reaches of pleasure and fulfillment. They resolve the transition crisis by giving up their heretofore stubborn illusions about who the other really is.

The Exceptional Marriage

> *This is my living faith, an active faith, a faith of verbs: to question, explore, experiment, experience, walk, run, dance, play, eat, love, learn, dare, taste, touch, smell, listen, argue, speak, write, read, draw, provoke, emote, scream, sin, repent, cry, kneel, pray, bow, rise, stand, look, laugh, cajole, create, con-*

front, confound, walk back, walk forward, circle, hide, seek. To seek: to embrace the questions, to be wary of the answers.

—*Terry Tempest Williams*

Couples who are able to reach this fourth stage are fortunate indeed! The Eros felt in stage one pales in comparison to the intimacy and deep abiding love that resides here. Exceptional couples really value each other and have moved beyond "parallel existence" into genuine enjoyment of each other's company. They have come to the realization that the marriage is a never-ending source of discovery, pleasure, and inspiration. This is not to paint a picture of a Disney World existence. The Exceptional Marriage still spends some of its time in survival consciousness. These couples are quite able, however, to open up to higher levels of connection and self-expression.

Exceptional couples have learned that in a life spent together there is a natural vacillation between the need for secure connection and the longing for adventure, exploration, and creative expression. Both states complement each other. Couples therapist and author Esther Perel (2006) refers to these as the "anchor and the wave." She quotes psychoanalyst Stephen Mitchell: "…we all need security: permanence, reliability, stability, and continuity. These rooting, nesting instincts ground us in our human experience. But we also have a need for novelty and change, generative forces that give life fullness and vibrancy."

Stage four couples are comfortable with a broader range of emotional expression. Anger, need, desire, fear, hurt, and love are all more readily expressed as couples begin to develop the courage to stand in truth. It is not always easy, but it is more likely to be real. In all relationships, the energy we give will ultimately equal the energy we receive. In stage four, there is a much higher energy quotient. The vibrancy quotient notches up. This is what we have been calling full self-expression.

There are six characteristics that define the Exceptional Marriage.

1. Unpredictability
2. Commitment
3. Mature need
4. Strength
5. Exceptional sex
6. Spirit

Unpredictability

The *sine qua non* of the Exceptional Marriage is the couples readiness, willingness, and ability to embrace unpredictability. When couples gain sufficient power through the crucible of the Transition Stage, they begin to open to each other in wide-eyed wonder. There is a dawning awareness of how little they truly knew about each other. It is not that they really didn't know, but that they were heretofore unwilling to fully absorb the truth of what was right there under their respective noses. Wittgenstein once wrote: "The aspects of things that are most important are hidden because of their simplicity and familiarity." He might have been telling us that in the Control Stage we have lost appreciation for the enormously and wondrously complex being that is our partner.

Before this final stage, not only do we fail to see, but we also fail to reveal. We don't see the mystery of our partner, and we don't display our own mystery. When we stay immersed and embedded in myth and habit, we see what we see, and we miss much. Because we never know for sure what lies beyond our preconceived, firmly established notions of reality, we must come to make love with unpredictability.

The exceptional couple continually breaks free of the shackles of habit. Gone is the inevitability of each other's actions. A good example of this is John and Tammy's relationship. John used to see Tammy as a complainer. She would express unhappiness with their lack of playtime on weekends. He was convinced that she was not taking life seriously enough and was being frivolous with their money. Recently, he began to realize that she was fun-loving and a great catalyst for change. He had to come to terms with his fear about letting go of responsibilities and spending money. Once he started to do this, Tammy became a great source of adventure and pleasure.

Unpredictability is the source from which creativity flows. Creative energy moves swiftly through uncharted airspace. Exceptional couples exude creative life force because they are not tying up their energy in defensive control patterns. The more each partner learns to express simple emotional truths, the more creativity is unleashed. This creative spirit is vital to fourth stage couples. When relationships are devoid of inventive, inspired expressive outlets, they languish is dull and dreary spaces. It is a sad marriage where no there is no song.

In the Exceptional Marriage, when one partner says "I'm unhappy" (generating a sense of uncertainty in the other), her spouse does not get defensive or try to make it all better. Instead, he wants to know why. Exceptional couples are willing to challenge the free-floating fret of the Control Stage, where the expression of unhappiness sets off alarm bells that mobilize an urgent effort to retract back to safe and familiar ground. Greater honesty breeds unpredictability. Exceptional couples welcome this. While it is still scary, it is also exhilarating. Commitment arises in exceptional relationships not from mutually "managed care" but from trust that emotional upheaval can lead to greater strength.

Commitment

To fully and openly commit oneself to another flawed human being is simultaneously the most terrifying and satisfying decision one may ever make. To be sure, the long-term relationship is a colossal challenge and not a path for every person. Commitment involves the merger of our self-preservation or autonomy drive with the recognition of the reality of our connectedness. As spiritual author Diarmuid

O'Murchu (1998) suggests, "Without this mutual interdependence, nothing attains its full potential."

Commitment to another is commitment to oneself. Our uniqueness and our sameness are honored together in what Marcia and I call radical commitment, which involves the full knowledge that we are more complete as individuals within the embrace of our relationship. Our unique gifts are best expressed through the intimacy of our shared life with this particular partner. This is not a fanciful notion of a pre-ordained "soul-mate," but rather a testimony to choice. Here, each spouse chooses to let the relationship be their source and ground for finding their deepest truths.

The exceptional couple has nearly extinguished the inner hesitancy to fully commit; this hesitancy is born out of either the fear of losing oneself or the dread of a broken heart. Unlike in the Control Stage, this commitment is a clear, unambiguous inner knowledge that says, "I'm not going anywhere. This is where I want to be."

Commitment in earlier stages is of a more primitive nature. These immature brands of commitment include:

Commitment of heroic obligation—This is characterized by a sense of noble duty to one's partner.
Commitment from immature need—This occurs when one or both partners are afraid to think about life without each other.
Erotic commitment—This grows out of the altered state of consciousness of the Eros Stage when two people cannot believe that anybody else could ever meet their needs like this person does.
Moral commitment—This encompasses the sense of "I made my bed, and now I must sleep in it." Or, "My faith would not allow me to consider leaving my partner."
Static commitment—This means, "I commit to what we have, but you better not change too much."

Radical commitment in the Exceptional Marriage is more organic and more a choice we make from the clarity of unconstrained love. As we learn to express our emotional truths more fully, we are no longer hypnotized by our myths. We are also softer and less afraid to trust. Radical commitment is more an awareness we finally arrive at: "I am with the person that I want to be with. I love this person with all his or her idiosyncrasies and imperfections. My fantasies of something better no longer carry any weight."

This does not mean that an occasional, tenuous foray back into transitional trepidation can't occur. But the doubt is quickly extinguished by the undeniable reality of radical commitment. It is precisely this commitment that allows exceptional couples to manage so much unpredictability. In fact, the only certainty in the Exceptional Marriage is commitment. This creates the holding ground for pleasure, excitement, conflict, risk-taking, and vulnerability to flourish. It allows for the possibility that the hormonal charge of the Eros Stage can be coupled with the oxytocin induced attachment of the early Control Stage. Through the crucible of commitment, wild and exciting things begin to happen. So much energy is freed up to be creative, to have fun, to love, to go out on a limb, and to give oneself fully to the wide, wonderful world out there.

Prior to stage four, commitment is more a promise. In stage four, it is a given. It just is. To get here, couples must pass through the gut-wrenching soul search of the Transition Stage. Exceptional couples cross into Stage Four with an answer: "This is the person I want share a seat with on the roller coaster of life."

Mature Need

If you recall from our discussion above, there are both mature and immature needs. While childhood needs are remnants from an earlier time in life, genuine adult needs emerge from the awakening of our consciousness. As we come to realize how much we are part of something larger than our puny selves, we open our eyes to how much we need. Our partners are the ones we need most, not for giving us what Mommy or Daddy failed to deliver, but as a source of courageous connection. It is highly courageous to acknowledge, "You matter to me." Often this realization causes such inner consternation that we become emotionally dismissive of our "beloved." Letting ourselves know just how much our partners do matter can cause us to go weak in the knees.

When couples are able to see each other in truth (neither idealizing nor demonizing), they are then open to feeling mature need. To allow ourselves to experience the full-bodied, wholly conscious, undefended need for our partner is high up on the list of peak experiences. To feel, to express, to reveal that "I need you" from the fullness of my heart and soul, transports me to the absolute highest reaches of the human experience. It is a thing of miraculous beauty. It is also scary as hell.

Need has routinely been relegated to the dung heap of human experience. But this is the result of a profound fear of vulnerability. In a need-phobic world, the grandest virtue is bootstrap autonomy. In such a world, need is misconstrued as a sign of weakness, a symptom of codependence, or an egocentric self-absorption. But exceptional couples know better. Real need is a shedding of all defenses. Feeling how important our partner is to us is humbling. Contact with this place may send a quiver of tender surrender through our very fiber. It is so much easier to, in marriage therapist David Schnarch's (1991) words, "live with a pain in the ass than with a pain in the heart."

The sweet pain of need is routinely rejected in favor of the hard pain of contraction or pulling away into faux autonomy. Exceptional couples are quite capable of surviving without each other. But they really understand, appreciate, and hold immense gratitude for how much better they each are together. Their "I need you" is not the desperate, demanding immature need of earlier stages. It is the fully aware knowledge that "With you, I am capable of so much more than without you." It is not a regressive need; it is transformative.

Strength

In an Exceptional Marriage, each partner celebrates the emerging strength of his or her spouse. This is radically different than couples in the Control Stage. In stage two, partners are highly competitive and are more apt to unconsciously desire failings in each other that allow them to feel superior. To feel "less than" is way too threatening.

Leisha constantly complains that Michael is unwilling to share his feelings with her and that he never expresses his need for her. When she finally dragged Michael to a couples' workshop, it was he that was more available and open. When Leisha witnessed this, it did not float her boat, instead she refused to believe it. She was threatened by his strength and the challenge to her myth of "Michael the Zombie."

Exceptional couples don't live in a fantasy world. Quite the contrary—fantasy resides in the domain of the Control Stage. Exceptional couples will quite regularly disagree, say the wrong thing, get hurt, or be disappointed. The difference is that their inner fortitude allows them to not take these occurrences to a code-red, high-level threat.

The strength in the Exceptional Marriage comes from two dovetailing sources. One is the growing maturity of each partner. As partners become more certain of who they are and how they feel, they will take this strength back into their interactions. Neither can push the other around, or get away with the games and the manipulations that worked so flawlessly in an earlier stage. Their energy is evenly matched, as in the case of Steve and Charlene. For years, Steve was able to convince Charlene that his low sexual desire was due to her being too inhibited in bed. Now Charlene is able to recognize that the problem is not a simple equation— "Because I have inhibitions, Steve is turned off." As she has gotten stronger, she doesn't blindly endorse Steve's version of their sexual problem. Likewise, Steve is now more able to see how he feels safer with Charlene when she holds her sexuality back. He has developed the strength to acknowledge his own sexual inhibitions. As each partner becomes increasingly more mature and self-aware, control patterns and linear blame cannot be sustained.

The second source of strength derives from the radical commitment that flourishes in stage four. Couples begin to trust the relationship's integrity enough to exhale and speak the truth. Conversations become more meaningful and freewheeling. Because of the commitment they feel toward each other, exceptional couples bring more passion to all their interactions. They don't always utilize the proper communication techniques or avoid all offending remarks. They are not constrained by political correctness. From time to time one or the other may be immature, inappropriate, boorish, crabby, constipated, pouty, bossy, or ruled by PMS. So what? This does not signal the demise of the relationship.

Likewise, one may go into a shell, have a hissy fit, stay out too late, or make the same stupid mistake that's been made a thousand times before. No longer do these prevarications call into question the very sanctity of the relationship. Exceptional couples know, "My partner's peculiarities are not indications of some grand crisis and are not really my concern. I don't have to like them, but I don't have to personalize them, either."

Exceptional Sex

Exceptional couples know that sex is an opportunity to be more fully expressive. Sex becomes an expression of deep connection, because that's where it wants to take us—if we allow it. Exceptional sex may not look like the popular notion of pulse-pounding, heart-throbbing, high-on-the-Richter Scale, orgasm-centric intercourse. While that scenario may occur, it is not the essence of exceptional sex. When couples have been married for ten, twenty, thirty, forty, or more years, sex must evolve along with the relationship. Therefore, there is no fixed image of exceptional sex.

At its core, exceptional sex is an adventure. Each time spouses come together, there is no way of knowing what will happen. Isn't this the essence of excitation? Couples who are willing to let their sex be a creative dance of the unknown have realized the vision. In exceptional marriages, couples live each day with an openness to change. So it is with their sex lives. Sex is the ultimate opportunity to discard the notion of predictability. Hence we are reintroduced to Eros, with the added benefit of authentic connection.

Exceptional sex isn't always joyous. Sometimes it may result in the emergence of some unspoken, unresolved hurt or a negativity that was begging to be addressed. Often, it allows us to touch our delicate fears of being seen in all our imperfection. Recently, during a session with a couple, the husband Mick shared this story: "Something very amazing happened to us last week. While we were having sex, I could feel Angie tense up. Normally I would get frustrated, roll over, and give up. This time, however, I asked her 'what's up?' She said she felt fear. I suggested to her to go into the fear. She began to cry deeply, then she laughed, then she came." This is as eloquent a description of exceptional sex as there is.

The great paradox of long-term relationships is that, in some very important way, we actually feel less safe and experience a sense of greater danger in self-exposure. This is because our partner becomes increasingly important to us; the stakes are higher. Thus, sex is most often avoided, not because of stress, lack of time, built-up resentment, weight gain, smelly armpits, or marauding kids, but because it feels safer to sidestep all the vulnerability associated with desire. To express desire is to say you are important!

Exceptional sex, even after our golden anniversary, is fraught with the wildness of unknowing. We must, however, be open to it, and that is the great catch. Most couples remain too afraid to deviate from their tried-and-true approaches to sexual intercourse. They opt for safety over vulnerability.

Sex is so vital to the Exceptional Marriage because it is the last bastion of meaningful nonverbal communication. Couples have become so dependent on the spoken word in order to relate that sex is often the only remaining way they connect from the waist down. Our axiom for couples is "less talk, more expression." Sex is powerfully expressive and a welcome oasis from the arid world of the spoken word.

Sexual energy and aggressive energy run on the same current. It's no coincidence that the phrase "fuck you" is used aggressively. Couples who have been together for a significant amount of time often lose the aggressive element to their sexuality. Healthy aggression in sex means to express your lust; it means to want, to make noise, to reach out, to squeeze, to thrash, to say dirty things to each other, to not be shy about asking for what you like, to dominate, to submit.

Aggression in sex fades for many reasons (aging, parenting, insecurity, control patterns, hormonal mysteries), but it does not disappear in an Exceptional Marriage. Aggression wilts when we try to take the risk out of sex. Sex will inevitably open us to discovering something new about ourselves and our partners. All emotions are, at one time or another, apt to be part of our sexual experience. Fear, vulnerability and aggression are familiar bedfellows in exceptional sex.

In the words of Perel, "Cleverly, our bodies remember what our minds may have chosen to forget, both light and dark. Perhaps this is why our deepest fears and most persistent longings emerge in intimate sex: the immensity of our neediness, the fear of desertion, the terror of being engulfed, the yearning for omnipotence."

As pharmaceutical companies inform us that considerable numbers of men suffer from ED or erectile dysfunction and can be helped by medication, it is worth asking what percentage of ED is related to the loss of aggressive sexual energy. Perhaps for some men, ED more accurately means "energy depletion or erotic disconnect." Marcia and I believe for both men and women that sexual apathy can often be overcome by reintroducing healthy aggression into the equation. Exceptional couples know this to be true.

Exceptional sex is intimacy intensive because it requires of its participants a willingness to be real. This stage isn't about performance; instead, exceptional sex asks us only to be authentic. Each sexual encounter will offer us the precious opportunity to let go of some phony, plastic, smiley-face place inside of us. When we are game for this adventure, we will share secrets, expose our desires, reveal our taboo fantasies, convey our insecurities in an undefended way, and let each other know what we want. Do you think this gets stale over time? Think again. Sex will get better as it evolves beyond the physical and embraces the deeply emotional and spiritual aspects of our humanity. Exceptional sex makes space for the raw and the refined.

Spirit

While the introduction of spirit into any discussion is fraught with complexity, we would be remiss if we ignored its significance to the Exceptional Marriage. In this context, we refer to spirit as the broad sense of being connected to a larger reality. This means having an awareness that there is more to life than we can presently know. As such, spirit is that part of us that is ever evolving and transforming. Exceptional couples are infused with a sense of spirit. Growing, expanding, deepening, and creating gives their lives meaning and purpose. The excitation of each new adventure is the essence of spirit in the Exceptional Marriage. Perhaps Gestalt therapy guru Fritz Perls (Quoted in Keen 1983) summed up the meaning of spirit best when he said, "I don't want to be saved, I want to be spent."

In its most simple and obvious manifestation, spirit is the quotient of aliveness that is experienced individually and mutually. Among control-based couples, one can easily notice the heaviness, stagnation, and stilted nature of their interactions. Conversely, exceptional couples generate more energy. They play on the edges of life. They operate with an abiding sense of connection to each other and to all existence. Their spirit is apparent not in their spoken beliefs but in their choices of how to live life. They are more magnanimous to each other in praise, in critical feedback, in revealing vulnerability, in touch, and in encouragement of risk-taking. As a couple, they are also more generous toward others. They are spiritual beacons in a world filled with fear and confusion about what it really means to be intimate. Their spirit is not defined by perfection but by life in all its grand imperfection.

There is one additional ingredient to our description of spirit in the Exceptional Marriage: vision. Exceptional couples know that life is not a pointless exercise. They understand that happiness is a byproduct of living in harmony with one's unique talents and gifts. In control stage, couples operate from a "have-to" model of life, in which couples are more reactive than proactive. They do what is required and never quite find a way to manifest their dreams. As a result they become misaligned. They live life wearing somebody else's shoes and another's hairstyle. On their deathbeds, someone else's life passes before their eyes. This living out of alignment with one's gifts and dreams is undoubtedly the greatest source of depression imaginable. No medication can cure this disease. It is a spiritual malady, not a biochemical one.

Conversely, the exceptional couple becomes more and more attuned to their own human strengths and gifts. They make choices that reflect a longing to express these personal qualities. This is the essence of vision. To inhabit this life with the yearning to fulfill one's potential establishes for each of us a personal vision. Couples who bring together their enormous individual resources will create a shared vision. This vision may be grand or small. It will perpetually take new form as couples evolve, but it always reflects a movement toward fulfilling potential. This is the opening to Full Self Expression.

Exceptional couples want to hear what each thinks and feels. In earlier stages, there is a very definite pressure to tailor what is said. Couples are cautious communicators. Marcia and I are not simply referring to constructive communication principles. Yes, how we say things is a vital part of the equation, but calculating our words does not make for full expression. In stage four, couples begin to speak much more from the heart. It is not so necessary to remember communication rules because the heart has no intention to harm. "Truth" spoken without love is no real truth. When two people are fully in love, they are not so afraid to say the wrong thing.

The expression of feelings may result from some distortion, but by bringing it out the fog lifts. Charlie, for instance, gets angry when Elizabeth fails to respond to his question. He thinks she is purposefully ignoring him. When she hears of his anger, and his belief that she's ignoring him, she clarifies for him why she was tuning him out. Elizabeth explains that she was preoccupied with a conversation she had earlier with a co-worker. In the past, Charlie would have said nothing because he thought he was being "irrational." Now, he expresses himself even when he is unsure. As a result, they both feel closer.

Full Self Expression

o o o o o o o o o o o o o o o o o o o o o o o

I love you, and because I love you, I would sooner have you hate me for telling you the truth than adore me for telling you lies.

—Pietro Aretino

For couples to shake off the doldrums of controlled interactions, they will need to cultivate full self-expression. Partners that are mired in their particular control patterns are disaffected from each other. Their range of human expression is seriously compromised, leaving a gaping hole where intimacy should be found.

Let's take a closer look at what we mean by full self-expression. As we described in Chapter One, the drive toward full self-expression complements the self-preservation drive. Whereas the self-preservation drive is utilized to keep us physically and psychologically intact, the drive toward self-expression pushes us toward our full capabilities. It is what distinguishes us from all other known life forms. Self-preservation is protective; self-expression is creative. Thus full self-expression, by nature, carries us into uncharted territory. This is the domain of the passionate, the vulnerable, and the unpredictable. The Exceptional Marriage is, above all else, the sacred ground of self-expression.

Self-expression is all about releasing what we hold back from our partners and the world. Bringing forth our creative aspirations, our salty sense of humor, our blubbering sentimentalism, our secret hostilities, our impossibly vulnerable thirst for love, and our unfathomable gratitude all involve releasing our controlled and measured demeanors.

To release is to sweat, to orgasm, to tremble, to soften the stiff upper lip. When Marcia and I talk about full self-expression, we are inviting you and your partner into a world of thunderstorms and rainbows where cruel intentions are kin to a caring heart. In the organicity of life, there is a time to hold and a time to release. Children are masters of release; adults are adept at holding. Neither are very good at the opposite. Full self-expression allows for the unvarnished release of passionate energy tempered only by the consciousness of mature love—a love that the child has yet to embrace.

As the dance of marriage settles into a tightly choreographed series of emotional two-steps, self-expression diminishes. Control patterns quell the fires of emotional and creative release. When we hunker down into narrow styles of relating to each other, we steel ourselves against the perceived susceptibility of the wide-open heart. As we retreat from the brilliant exposure to love, we hide in the gloom of our myths and control patterns. The final destination for most couples is the hardened space of mutual blame or vacant coexistence. The road back to a wide-open heart and pure love takes us through increasingly vulnerable expressions of various emotional states. This is what we call full self-expression.

Critics of emotional release work tell us that expressing so-called negative emotions is at best useless and most likely harmful. This is essentially true if the only thing that happen is couples expressing mutual blame. The expression of blame alone is a meager release indeed. In full self-expression, we do not shy away from the human reality that most conflict begins with blame and that its expression can be a gateway to a richer emotional exchange. When couples remain deadlocked in blame, then all of the criticisms are merited.

Opponents of emotional release suggest that the "anything goes" approach is detrimental to human relationship. We agree, because "anything goes" implies that we can dump our anger on our spouse and leave it at that. Full self-expression does not endorse "anything goes" but replaces it with "going all the way." In order to open your heart, it is often (though not always) necessary to express all that clutters its path. "Going all the way" means we don't stop after satisfying the urge to blame. We must also be willing to come to our partner with our own selfishness, cruelty, self-affirming anger, fears, hurts, needs, remorse, and gratitude. The intention behind full self-expression is to uncover our love for our partner. We must give everything, not just anything. It is a hero's journey into the jaws of vulnerability and the bosom of intimacy.

Marriage—indeed, life—is an intense experience. We desperately try to convince ourselves otherwise, but to fully reside on this planet requires a befriending of extremes. Psychologist Michel Eigen (1996) describes it this way: "Emptying out feeling, emptying out thought, emptying out energy versus hyperfeeling, hyperthinking, hyperenergy: going through extremes is an important part of life. Extreme states add intensity, diversity, and richness to living ... Intensity nourishes us, waters our bodies and beings."

Biologically, it also may well be that an ability to express strong emotions is helpful in allowing one to drop into more connective, vulnerable feelings. Psychologist Carolyn Zahn-Waxler (Quoted in Rosenthal 2002) "suggests that low levels of empathy may be related to low activity levels in the sympathetic nervous system."

When couples can express anger, it tends to increase each partner's sympathetic "fight-or-flight" response. By activating the nervous system, we might actually be supporting the internal conditions for empathy. To put it more simply, if we can fight, we can have compassion.

In this chapter, we will explore how couples can learn to deepen their connection and unlock their potential through a process of full self-expression. We have laid out a map for traversing through all of the layers of reactions that occur in intimate relationships. All of us have buried our primary restorative reactions behind a complicated array of control patterns and myths. As a result, full self-expression requires a process of dropping deeper into our core through increasing exposure of all of what we hold inside.

In our mentoring work with couples, we utilize the following process as a template for full self-expression. The whole point is to bring couples closer together, and emotional expressiveness is the glue. Because our essential aliveness is characterized by uncertainty and unpredictability, it rarely (probably never) unfolds as it is laid out here. We also want to note that we are emphasizing the spoken word in this description, but in our actual work, we rely a great deal on touch, movement, and nonverbal vocal expression such as yelling, growling, sighing and numerous other forms of vocalization.. Words alone are not nearly enough.

This model is used with couples who are stuck in control styles of relating or who have moved into the crisis of the Transition Stage. The purpose is to assist them in getting to the truth of what keeps them separate and unable to contact each other in a more genuine way. Occasionally this means finding out that they do not want each other. Mostly, however, it gives them an opportunity for a level of intimacy they have never before experienced.

The eleven layers are broken down into two components: intensifying energies and releasing energies. In body oriented psychotherapies such as Core Energetics, this is referred to as charge and discharge. Intensifying energies bolster our autonomy, while releasing energies allow us to surrender into intimacy. Sometimes these energies are referred to as "masculine" and "feminine." Marcia and I prefer to leave out any reference to gender because it seems to miss the mark. We all possess both the so-called masculine and feminine aspects, and gender distinction only confuses the reality.

It is frequently necessary to intensify or build up energy between partners before release or softening occurs. It is most often the case that emotions need to be "matched." For one partner to be openhearted and loving while the other is angry is a mismatch. Relationships adore energetic equilibrium. Intensifying energy wants to be met with equivalent intensity. This is why one spouse will prod another into greater reaction. There is pleasure in having our energy fully met by our partner's. Energy that is "matched" can then release itself. Thus full self-expression takes us from most defended to most vulnerable, from rigid self-preservation to a fluid manifestation of love's unbridled passion. For without anger there is no passion; without hurt there is no empathy; without fear there is no nurturing.

In this formulation, we are indebted to John Pierrakos and his model of Core Energetics. Dr. Pierrakos helped to bridge the body-mind gap in psychotherapy. In Core Energetics, we learn that "lower self" energies need to be owned with consciousness before the "higher self" can take its rightful place. Through the lectures of Eva Pierrakos, Marcia and I learned about the significance of avoiding our emotional truths and how we cannot grow spiritually until we have claimed all of our emotions. Alexander Lowen gave us the gift of his extensive writings on energy, emotions, and the body. Wilhelm Reich had the courage to first confront the lack of emotional and sexual expression in the treatment room. Finally, John Gray gave us his brilliant construction of the Total Truth Process. In his Total Truth Process, Dr. Gray (2002) clearly lays out five steps for moving from anger to love. Full self-expression is a synthesis, expansion, and evolution of the work of these teachers and many others coupled with what we have come to know through our own experience.

Full self-expression is not a technique to be applied mechanically. Though sometimes Marcia and I will encourage couples to consciously go through each layer, the value of full self-expression lies more in building awareness about the human emotional reality. In a sense, it is a cartography of emotional relationship. We can spend time discovering hidden truths in each and every one of the eleven layers.

This model is constructed on the bedrock of personal responsibility. Unless each partner is at least willing to hold a positive intention to see his or her part in the relationship drama, full self-expression cannot unfold. Many couples are not ready to express such intense and taboo feelings, yet even the most controlled couples can benefit by gently being exposed to aspects of their emotional lives that lay dormant and exiled from awareness. With this in mind, let's take a look at the various layers of full self-expression.

Expression of "Intensifying Energies"

1. Expressing blame and judgment
2. Taking ownership of childhood needs
3. Owning one's desire to hate, to hurt, to demean, and to punish a spouse
4. Acknowledging and energizing resistance to restorative feelings
5. Using nonverbal expression (releasing energy through sound & movement)
6. Expressing self-affirming anger

Expression of "Releasing Energies"

7. Revealing and dispelling fears of abandonment
8. Expressing hurt
9. Expressing remorse and personal responsibility
10. Opening to feeling mature need and longing
11. Expressing love, appreciation, radical commitment and positive intent

1. Expressing Blame

Blame is the universal control pattern employed by nearly all couples in their disputes. We all learn to blame others (or ourselves) at a young age so as not to feel our primary emotions. Witness the child who learns to say "bad chair" when he stubs his toe against it. Fault-finding is easier than dealing with the emotions that exist underneath. For many of us, it is almost a knee jerk reaction to affix liability to our spouse. One partner says to another, "You must have moved my keys; I know I left them right here." It is so tempting to pass the buck in this way that it often comes gushing out.

Blame by its very nature is motivated by a resistance to change oneself and a fixation on easily digested answers. Genuine responsibility, on the other hand, requires us to look more deeply at ourselves and to take ownership of our part in a mutual struggle. We take responsibility from a place of compassion for ourselves and for our partners. We blame from a place of rejection. We affix blame, but we accept responsibility. Blame invites humiliation, while responsibility invokes humility. One way to detect blame is by its simplistic characterizations. Stupid, lazy, bad with money, lousy lover, selfish, clumsy, and so on are the crude frames we place around each other to define the problem.

The most common reason for blaming our partners is to avoid blaming ourselves. If you moved my keys, then I can sidestep my own self-criticisms about being so disorganized. Our partners are the ideal candidates for slamming us with our own worst self-judgments. His criticism of her will mirror her self-blame. Her self-blame will trigger her blame of him, and so on. This sets the stage for a "War of the Roses" type battle. Blame begetting blame.

This attachment to blame is the outgrowth of a myth of perfection. Every one of us has character styles that result in our making the same mistakes over and over. Yet somehow we develop a myth that we should be able to purge ourselves of these flaws. So, too, should our partners be able to change their characteristic shortcomings. We tend to find fault in ourselves or our spouse rather than compassionately acknowledging each of our shortcomings. This is a hard habit to break.

Another component of blame, as we have already described, is the distortion of cause and effect. In our desire to have simple answers, we apply linear cause and effect descriptions to our human interactions. When Bart says to Evelyn, "If you would just show more interest in sex, I wouldn't flirt with your girlfriends," he is operating from this "cause and effect" distortion. He's saying, "I am the way I am because of you." Evelyn, conversely, will say, "I shut down to you sexually because you make me feel so threatened." She, too, is convinced that this is really the crux of the situation. Bart, in her mind, is the cause of her shutting down sexually. Both arguments make sense and are held as absolute truths by each spouse. But, as we discussed in our description of shared energy, human relationships do not operate this way. Who caused the problem is not only an irrelevant question, it is also unknowable. In all likelihood, Bart is flirtatious for a variety of motives and Evelyn is withholding for her own array of reasons. There may be a partial truth in their accusations, which is what gives blame its power. We take the kernel of truth and turn it into a cornfield. We become convinced that if our partners would just change, all would be well.

This tendency to pigeonhole human interaction into cause-and-effect equations weakens us in ways we do not fully comprehend. By blaming you, I have to hold the myth that I am only a reactor to life. I cannot be a creator or initiator. I render myself a mere effect. Every time I imply that the situation we're in is your fault, I relinquish my authority and grant you ultimate control.

Yet, in spite of the problems blame creates, it is not all bad. Because we live in a culture that thrives on blame (just listen to any political discourse), we can count on fault-finding as a fact of married life. Our narratives are saturated with blaming dialogue. It can't be helped. Blaming can serve a larger purpose if we are to willing to receive it back after we dish it out. Unless we can take it, we do not possess the moral authority to give it.

In very few places in this world will you be confronted with your shortcomings as you will in your marriage. The germ of truth in every blaming statement can challenge us to look a bit deeper at whom we really are. While we could say it in more constructive ways, and we need to put each blaming statement in its proper context, it is often through our partner's criticisms of us that we discover some aspect of ourselves we have been unaware of. So, while we can get bruised and battered by our blame exchanges, we can also find the elixir in the poison.

In the full self-expression process, we invite couples to bring their blaming to the surface. Because they may not initially be aware that they are blaming, we find that it is important to "name the beast." Much of the literature on communication suggests that we can overcome the tendency to blame simply by recognizing it and choosing not to do it anymore. Were it so easy! In the full self-expression process, we make room for couples to take ownership of their blaming and express it consciously as a first step toward moving into deeper levels of revealing. We will, for example, have a couple take turns saying "It's your fault!" and "You're to blame because …" Each partner can fully express all the ways she or he blames the other as a way to bring to awareness the full extent of the blame cycle. While good communication requires that we make "I" statements, in this first stage of full self-expression, we allow couples to indulge in making each other the problem.

Do any of these sound familiar?

- "You always/never …"
- "You're more interested in your job than me."
- "You're never satisfied."
- "All you care about is sex."
- "You never tell me your feelings."
- "You spend too much."

- "You don't pull your weight around here."
- "You take me for granted."
- "You always reject my sexual advances."
- "You choose your friends or family over me."
- Blame disguised as question: "How come you don't ever see the mess in the bathroom?"

We need to emphasize here that while we encourage each person to take ownership of their blaming, this is done with the intent of moving into what is underneath. We have found that people are so energetically attached to blame that unless they can "air it out," they will strongly resist going to other levels. The only requirement here is that each partner own what they are expressing as blame.

Most of us are raised to believe that faultfinding gives us answers. It doesn't. From the myth of blame, we are left with the uncomfortable proposition that it's either you or me. Blame out or blame in. There is a huge distinction between blame and personal responsibility. Blame is narrow; self-responsibility is wide. Blame is tough; self-responsibility is tender. Self-responsibility encompasses compassion and humility. It also involves recognizing the broader reality. It says, "I have a role in this struggle, but I am not the whole problem."

Yet before we can take personal responsibility—way before in many cases—we often need to have our blame. In our mentoring work, we do not simply have couples verbalize their blame, we also have them express it through their bodies. This typically means that they need to physically move their bodies to release the tension that coincides with blaming and defending. For instance, we may have a wife punch down on pillows while shouting, "It's your fault our son is failing!" followed by the husband hitting the pillows and shouting, "If you weren't such a bitch he wouldn't be so rebellious!"

When couples know that we are giving them space to indulge in their blaming, it creates sufficient safety to express these silent criticisms. The couple with the failing son may have never said outright that they blame each other, but it is obvious in their more subtle criticisms. By exposing the full extent of their blaming, it allows them to first begin to release frustration and then to express what else lies underneath.

2. Owning our childhood needs

Childhood needs involve the expectations we all place upon our spouses to make up for some childhood deficit. They reflect our own egocentricity. Childhood needs are really thinly veiled demands. In our unspoken demands of our partner, we hold certain fantasies and expectations of them that never quite get revealed. It has been said that expectations are resentments under construction. When the childhood need is not met, the "negligent spouse" is held accountable for the sins of the "needy spouse's" parents.

Most of us who are married feel the pressure to be more than who we are. We accept the premise that somehow it is up to us to take care of our spouse without ever challenging the value in doing so. In their relationship Sage always drops what she is doing when Carl expresses a need for attention. She never considers that if she says "no," Carl will manage without her. Sage believes that she is being a good wife but fails to recognize that Carl's need for attention is not coming from his mature adult consciousness, but rather from an unmet childhood need which was legitimate when he was six but is not real as a grownup. For Carl it is more an expectation than an honest and vulnerable request for attention.

Couples are largely unaware of the nature and strength of their childhood needs. They may not even express them overtly. But the existence of the childhood needs generates an insidious strain within the relationship that deprives each person the capacity to fully love the other. Providing surrogate parenting to your spouse does not qualify as mature love, nor does it serve your spouse. It is not our job to rescue each other from the dungeons of the past.

In full self-expression, we want couples to bring to awareness the nature of their respective childhood needs. By expressing them directly, couples begin to see the absurdity and impossibility of meeting them. Also, by airing them out, they lose their emotional charge. We want couples to become completely aware of the demands they place upon each other. Frequently, when they do so, the tension between them disappears and they feel safer and more loving toward each other.

As with the expression of blame, in a mentoring session we will support couples in revealing their childish demands with great fervor. By putting them out with the full intensity with which they are felt, couples are able to let go of the grip these childhood needs have.

For example, partners may express statements such as these:

- "It's your job to make me feel secure."

- "You have to make me feel attractive."

- "You can't have needs."

- "You must always be strong."

- "It's your job to make love to me whenever I want you to."

- "You had better not criticize me."

- "It's your job to stay home make me meals and make sure the kids don't bother me."

- "You have to make lots of money so I don't have to ever worry about having what I want."

- "I need you to always take my side when I have a conflict with friends or family."

- "I want you to leave me alone—unless I call for you. Then come running."

When couples really get into the spirit of expressing their childhood needs, they may take pleasure in stretching them to the height of self-centeredness. Sometimes we encourage couples to be as outrageous as possible, with demands such as, "I want you be my love slave, feeding me grapes and washing my feet, then giving me oral sex. Then you can leave and take care of all the chores while I relax!" By revealing these selfish fantasies, which extend even beyond the actual childhood need, couples often get a laugh at seeing this side of each other.

The point of expressing our childhood needs is to bring us closer. Also, we become more aware of how we actually hold these demands in day-to-day life. The more we are able to reveal our private childhood needs, the closer we come to having our mature needs met. The moment my partner is privy to my hidden demands and fantasies, we make deeper connection, and this is our real, mature need. Finally, there are those times in relationships where each spouse's child-self shows up and could use some love, attention and acceptance. When partners can acknowledge that this is occurring one can honestly ask for support and the other can freely give it.

3. Owning the desire to hate, to hurt, to demean and to punish.

A few words of warning: What you are about to read is the subject of significant controversy. As we've noted, the prevailing belief on the subject of expressing anger is that it's a bad idea. According to this argument, expressing anger foments more anger. Therefore, the solution to anger is to purge oneself of it before it decimates your marriage. Many of these types of suggestions amount to glorified versions of counting to ten and breathing away this nasty feeling.

Our belief is that it is the *inappropriate* expression of anger—done without taking ownership—that leads to the fear and confusion about emotional release work. As you read this chapter, you will notice that there are different manifestations of anger in the first few stages of the full self-expression process. We have called this "intensifying" our energy. We see this emotion as having three main variations: blame, destructive anger, and self-affirming anger. Each needs to be distinguished for what it is.

Our work with couples involves releasing anger as a pathway to love. Each person must understand that their destructive energy (which is clearly part of every relationship) can only be expressed in service of finding the love. Unless each partner has the positive intention to love, there is no good that will come from expression of destructive anger. Exceptional marriages are able to grow from the turbulent tirades of appropriately expressed anger. We acknowledge that many couples are not ready for the honest expression of volatile feelings. But we have come to believe that marriages cannot reach the Exceptional Stage until they can embrace these potent forces that are lurking in the shadows.

One of the most perilous places to travel in the long-term relationship is into the realm of our destructiveness. This is such a terrifying undertaking that it is almost universally avoided. The vast majority of spouses are not even conscious of the negativity that each possesses. We frequently hear from couples we work with, "I don't hate him," or "I would never want to hurt her." While this is ultimately true, it is also true that, at certain moments, cruelty, hate, and destructiveness do exist. The absence of awareness does not make this less of a reality.

None of us wishes to believe that we hold an intention to be mean, hurtful, or threatening to our spouse. If we do not find these places within us, however, we can create a civil, cordial relationship, but we cannot evolve into the Exceptional Marriage. Love and hate are not such strange bedfellows. It is life's greatest paradox that the more somebody matters to us, the more of a hazard they pose. The most dangerous person to me is the one I love most.

In life there are two primary positions: being separate or being connected. Our destructiveness (or what is referred to as the lower self) emerges from separation. We want to stay separate whenever feeling connected becomes too threatening. The more connected or loving we feel, the more vulnerable we believe we are. Thus we want to hurt, demean, or destroy to feel the presumed safety of separation. Yet true safety only exists in connection. So we live with the dilemma of longing for connection while feeling terrified of loving. Our truly negative impulses are there to preemptively keep someone from harming us. Love brings to the surface every emotion unlike itself.

In marriage we cannot possibly feel our complete capacity for love without taking responsibility for our lower self. Full self-expression includes the willingness to find and expose this negative place within. This means being able to acknowledge and express all the ways we want our spouse to suffer, to feel shame, to feel rejected by us, to be scared of us, and even to perish.

In the mentoring process, we encourage the expression of this lower-self negativity. The expression of the destructive desire is the best way to divest ourselves of the power such negativity holds over us. By holding it back, we miss the opportunity to open the door to intimacy. True, the expression of destructive feelings is fraught with risk. Couples need to learn to do this in the presence of supportive mentors, at least initially, until they are assured that such expression won't escalate into harmful exchanges.

Probably the intent to harm is a variant of the "fight or flight" response. In certain choice moments, we want to kill off our tormentors or at least punish them and make them feel bad. We have a secret tormentor within us, but we'll never confess to it. This is precisely why full self-expression requires that each person brings forth his or her lower self.

In our mentoring work, Marcia and I will have couples take turns blowing out the build up of negative energy. This will almost always require bodily release. Just as a child may stomp around saying, "I hate you," adults too need to physically and verbally express our intense feelings. Nobody wants to encourage children to be violent, hateful creatures, but all of us have a physiological need to release our aggression. In the full self-expression process, we create a safe way for couples to discharge volatile emotions. Thus, yelling and hitting soft objects allows for the body to come back to balance.

During this work we will often hear such phrases as:

- "I hate you!"
- "I want you to feel like shit!"
- "Go to hell!"
- "I want to kill you!"
- "I hope you fail!"
- "I want to humiliate you!"
- "I'll make you pay!"

There are numerous (and sometimes expletive-saturated) variations of these phrases, but the common link is the desire to hurt one's partner. Notice the difference in these exclamations compared to the blaming statements listed earlier. Here, we are taking ownership through "I" statements. These negative "I" statements allow us to acknowledge and release our cruelty without having to act it out. Often our blaming statements hold a hidden cruel intent. If we honestly own our malice, we actually create greater safety in our marriage. When couples express their destructive feelings, it can be scary at first, but there is also a sense of relief. This relief happens both from expressing as well as from hearing one's partner express the concealed cruelties.

4. Refusing to feel restorative reactions

Little boys are sissies if they cry. Little girls are not ladylike if they get angry. We're all scaredy-cats if we admit to fear. We learn to feel shame at our primary feelings and our need for love and connection. We don't want to give up our long-cultivated, highly polished veneer of invulnerability. We resist dropping beneath the blame, the demands, and the lower-self hostility. To feel our hurts, fears, and needs seems too damned risky.

Through our personal narratives, we create myths that instruct us against exposing our vulnerable feelings. Typical myths include:

- "Others can't handle my feelings."
- "My tears will never stop if I let them out."
- "I don't have a right to feel hurt, or angry, or disappointed, etc."
- "Nobody cares."
- "If I express my feelings, you'll use them against me."
- "I don't have any feelings."
- "If I express my hurt, you'll only respond out of guilt."
- "Reason is more important than emotion."

Such myths lead us to regulate, modify, diminish, or totally negate our emotional truths. If we disallow our expression of our vulnerable feelings, then we become two-dimensional. We forfeit our mystery, nuance, soulfulness, and capacity to form deep attachments. It is amazing that we are willing to give so much up in the name of self-preservation.

To give an example, Ted never lets Carla know how hurt he feels when she rejects him sexually. His myth tells him, "If I expose my hurt, she'll think I'm insensitive to her right to say no." Gradually his heart shuts down and he settles for evenings of channel surfing. Most myths have some basis in truth. Carla may indeed get defensive and tell Ted he's insensitive for not understanding her. The likelihood that he accepts her definition suggests, however, that he has carried this myth with him into his marriage. It predated Carla's response.

Most of us believe it's not safe to feel or even that we can't feel these vulnerable emotions. It escapes us that we are actually refusing to surrender to emotions that create exposure and consequent vulnerability. In this fourth step, couples are invited to claim and exhibit their resistance and refusal to express these feelings. The energy of resistance is powerful. Anytime a partner feels pressured to express vulnerable emotions, be assured that there will be stubborn resistance. For one, we need to fully claim our autonomy before we can drop into intimacy. For another, we cannot simply feel on command.

We will never say "yes" until we are free to say "no," at least not honestly. Surrender always has to be on one's own terms. Marcia and I therefore encourage couples to express the place that says, in essence, "You can't have all of me!" Generally, when partners can indulge in this energy, they feel great pleasure. Such pleasure is a doorway to surrender. Sometimes a partner will need to remain in this place of resistance for quite awhile. The integrity of truth knows no timetable. We give full permission to say, "No, no a thousand times no!" Surrender, or discharge, will only occur when resistance has run its course and a partner organically feels ready to reveal more tender places. Often, there is a subtle judgment in therapy that says, "If you don't cry, you're hiding something." But "performance tears" accomplish nothing and will never result in full self-expression.

So we encourage spouses to move out their resistance with lines such as:

- "I won't show you my feelings!"
- "I don't trust you with my feelings."
- "You'll never get it from me!"
- "I'd rather die than show you that you matter!"
- "I refuse to be hurt by you!"
- "I won't give you the power!"

Doing this serves the twofold purpose of releasing the energy of resistance and of taking responsibility for an unwillingness to get vulnerable. All subsequent stages in this full self-expression model clue one's partner in to how much she matters. As you release into these feelings, hearts begin to soften, allowing for deeper connection.

5. Using Nonverbal Expression

Though this step is difficult to describe adequately, we include it here because it is fundamental to full self-expression. The bias toward the spoken word in the counseling room is a therapeutic cul-de-sac. Words alone do not create intimacy. The vast majority of communication between couples happens in their bodies, not their linguistic minds. In our mentoring work, Marcia and I routinely will support couples in revealing themselves through movement, breath, and nonverbal sound. It is actually not a separate step but can be part of the expression of any other emotion. We are not interested in just having partners say words to each other.

Physical release of the corresponding tensions and emotional energies is essential to complete the process. To say, for instance, "All the problems in our marriage are your fault" in a monotone voice does nothing to transcend the impulse to blame. Remember the goal here is to charge and discharge energy so that we feel closer. We don't feel closer simply by mouthing words.

There are literally hundreds of options for nonverbal expression, which we will not attempt to enumerate here. But we will offer some illustrations so you know what we mean.

- Encouraging a spouse to raise or soften her voice
- Having a couple make angry gestures and sounds
- One partner reaching out in a gesture of need for the other
- Dancing to music

- Thrusting pelvises at each other
- Having a dominant partner kneel in submission before his spouse
- Playing tug-o-war with a towel
- Receiving touch
- One partner singing to the other partner
- Flirting with only body language
- Having a spouse turn her back on a partner who is demanding attention
- Standing and wagging the finger of blame

The body speaks a language more ancient and sophisticated than Latin. Full self-expression requires physical build-up and release of the energies that are being denied between spouses. It is often the most effective way to get couples to drop their control patterns with each other.

For example, in a mentoring session, Tina and Luis were offered the opportunity to play out one of their control patterns. Tina grew up having to be a parent to her two younger siblings. Early on she stopped asking for anything because she was hurt by her parent's unavailability. In her marriage, she finds it impossible to just ask Luis for help, so instead she barks instructions. Luis is afraid to reveal his upset at being bossed around by his wife. As a child, he was routinely controlled by his older siblings.

Their control pattern involved Tina's demands and Luis' compliance. So we invited them to express their pattern energetically. Tina put her hands on her hips, hardened the features in her face, and ran off a litany of chores she expected him to do. Luis stood before her with a smile on his face and nodded in a "yes, dear" fashion while giving her "the finger" with both hands at his sides. By escalating her demanding tone and revealing his passive-aggressiveness, this couple became more open to connecting to their restorative emotions—for her the hurt and need; for him his self-affirming anger.

Nonverbal expression can be dramatic and explosive or dramatic and subtle. Lily and Herm, another couple Marcia and I mentored, had descended into a control pattern where he leaned on her as the strong one and she kept him at arms length because she pigeonholed him as inadequate. We suggested that he stand in front of her and place his hands on her shoulders. When we inquired how this felt to her, she said she wanted to collapse. His hands felt heavy, and she experienced him as a burden. She could see how this was a pattern in her life, as she had been expected to care for her younger brothers.

Herm was indeed leaning on her when he put his hands on her shoulders, playing out in a nonverbal way his demand to be held up. We then had him place his hands behind her neck and very gently draw her in his direction. We encouraged him to send a message through his hands that said to her, "I got you. I'll take care of you." Almost immediately, Lily melted into tears. She said she never had the experience of being taken care of like this before.

6. Expressing Self-Affirming Anger

For all the consternation surrounding the expression of anger, it holds a vital place in our process of growth and change. It is not far-fetched to say there is no "me" without anger. What Marcia and I call self-affirming anger is the true energy of human autonomy. Though there is much resistance to this idea, the boundary between self and other is sustained in an atmosphere of self-affirming anger. What Marcia and I are saying is that there is a great deal of predatory energy in this world—people willing to swallow you up if you allow them. Without expressing your self-affirming anger, there would soon be nothing left of you.

To express such anger is liberating. But people try to neuter anger by describing it in distilled terminology. We may hear that someone is "bothered," "perturbed," "distressed," "annoyed," or "upset" when they really are plain angry. Or a spouse may employ emotional sleight of hand by saying, "I'm really hurt by what you did," in a clearly hostile tone. This is emotional doublespeak, and it confounds the energetic reality. While the attempt may be to soften the edges of anger by using words that suggest milder reactions or different feelings altogether, it is almost always better to be direct.

Another diversionary tactic, as the inspired marriage therapist Julie Rosen so aptly pointed out, is to frame hostility in the form of a question. "Where were you?" is usually nothing more than anger camouflaged with a question mark. Many questions are thinly veiled accusations. "Do you really want to wear that sweater?" means "I hate how you look in that thing!"

When was the last time you heard your spouse simply say, "I'm angry with you"? Though we really would rather not hear such words, at least they are refreshingly up-front. Self-affirming anger, unlike blame, means taking ownership of your feelings, and unlike destructive anger, its purpose is not to harm, belittle, or intimidate the other, but rather to establish and secure your autonomy.

In the full self-expression model, we encourage partners to come forth with their self-affirming anger, and it can be a beautiful thing to behold! To stand up for oneself cleanly, unapologetically, and without malice is anger as it is meant to be. Self-affirming anger is about genuine power. When power meets power in a marital relationship, great things usually result. Often we hold back our power because we are fearful we'll blow our partners away. We don't give them credit for being able to handle our intensity. When we protect our partners, we compromise our capacity for a full relationship.

What we want most deeply is someone who doesn't shy away from our self-affirming anger. Children learn early on when a parent cannot tolerate anger and soon enough develop a control pattern of avoidance. Kids literally learn to protect parents in order not to lose them. This gets played out with regularity in our marriages.

In a mentoring session, we encourage the expression of self-affirming anger with such statement as:

- "I'm angry that you didn't call."
- "I get really upset when you expect me to pick up after you."
- "I want you to show me that you appreciate me.
- "I hate it when you talk to your family about me!"

7. Revealing and releasing fears of abandonment.

Most humans will go to great lengths not to feel fear. Using television, car radios, the Internet, and cell phones, we douse ourselves with a steady stream of human chatter. In our empty, quiet moments, fear can creep in. Paradoxically, as we begin to experience our own autonomy, fear sets up shop in the recesses of our limbic brain. Once a child knows he is a separate self, it dawns on him that he could be left alone. The wealth of literature on attachment reveals in no uncertain terms that young ones of many species, if left alone for too long, exhibit very distinct signs of terror and trauma. Fear is inextricably linked to isolation. The funny thing about autonomy is that it lets us know how truly dependent on each other we are. If you recall the movie *Castaway*, there is the indelible image of lonely Tom Hanks bonding with his volleyball "friend" Wilson and experiencing bona fide grief when the ball floats away on the ocean.

As we have mentioned, anger is a biological "fight or flight" reaction to threat. Its root system is made up of fear. Susan M. Johnson, (1996) creator of Emotionally Focused Marital Therapy, tells us, "Distressed couples are most often engaged in a process of seeking security and contact in the face of perceived danger and a threat to their relationship. Angry criticism is often most usefully viewed, then, as an attempt to modify the other partner's inaccessibility and as a *protest response to isolation and abandonment by the partner.*"

The awareness that you could lose your spouse generally doesn't get a great deal of airtime in day-to-day consciousness. A quivering little voice inside says, "Let's not go there," each time you are forced to consider the possibility. The fear of abandonment is the Swamp Thing in our placid pool of marital security. It's profoundly creepy as it emerges from the murkiness and stalks us.

When we begin to move out of our intense "autonomy-enhancing" emotions, it is often fear that greets us. Once we expend our aggressive reactions, we begin to feel our vulnerability. We peek into the place where relationship resides. To hold such fear means that our partners must truly matter to us. I get scared that you could hurt me or leave me. Owning my fear means admitting you matter. When we get a whiff of this sentiment, we move beyond energetic charge and the swagger of autonomy into the uncertain prospect of bona fide intimacy. It's enough to make us want to go hide behind our mommy's skirt.

In a sense, we drop down from the wounding to our ego, which is united with the autonomy-enhancing expressions, to the wounding of the heart that occurs with the intimacy-enhancing emotions. So in the process of full self-expression, we choose to reveal to our loved one our fears of abandonment. Typically, couples are not ready to drop into contact with this fear until they have indulged themselves adequately in the autonomous, intensifying emotions. When it does happen, though, the energy in the room shifts as emotional release begins. The acknowledgement of fear opens a door to the heart. Fear is an admission that a relationship exists and that one partner is important to the other. This awareness will often thaw a spouse's defensiveness.

We encourage partners to share the truth of their fears with each other using such language as:

- "I'm afraid that you hate me."

- "I m scared that we'll never get through this."

- "I am frightened that you find me unattractive."

- "It scares me to think that you might go away."
- "I'm terrified that my heart will stay shut."

Openness in revealing these dreaded places often has a powerful influence on one's spouse. It is a gesture saturated in humility and steeped in vulnerability when you give your partner this truth. There is no guile in the expression of fear. It is innocence supreme. Everything in the shared energy field begins to shift once fear is revealed. The gateway to even greater tenderness is flung open.

8. Expressing Hurt

Isn't it touching to see a child express her hurt so freely? Children are so damned susceptible to being hurt. We want to protect them, hold them, and make the hurt disappear. But we've learned to deny our own hurts as adults. We have dulled our emotional responsiveness to criticism, rejection, and ridicule. The school of hard knocks teaches us well. Instead of feeling the intensity of our pain, we steel ourselves energetically by tightening our muscles and creating myths in our minds.

A child who is regularly criticized will hold back hurt by tightening against its release. He will then create a myth to explain away the discordance in his head. He might say, "Dad is only telling me this for my own good." He might even create a narrative that holds some truth. "My father is a jerk" is easier to swallow than "It hurts so much that my father told me I was a loser."

The narrative we create is a useful filtering process that comes in handy in many areas of life. In marriage, however, hurts not expressed transmute into the bitterness of a hardened heart. Hurt is the primary restorative feeling that prompts us to remember how important our partner is to us. Sticks and stones may break our bones, but our partners can break our hearts.

To allow ourselves to be hurt by our partner's words or actions is to give them power. To have a truly Exceptional Marriage, we must grant them such power. While outwardly all couples clamor for intimacy, we are universally naïve about what it truly means. To let a partner matter so much that her criticism, disappointment, or rejection can make us recoil in pain isn't the brand of intimacy we signed on for. We refuse to accept that anguish and Eros are the conjoined twins of passionate engagement; that to live in a world where we can be deeply affected leaves us dangling between hell and hallowed ground. When we remove the filters and reveal our hurts, the seeds of intimacy have sprouted.

There is no full self-expression without the revelation of our hurts. Generally, couples cannot access their respective hurts until they have had permission to move out the charged up expressions of anger. But when they have come this far, it is crucial for each spouse to reveal their hurts. We encourage each person to do this with statements such as:

- "It hurts me when you point out my mistakes."

- "I feel really sad when you get so caught up in work that you ignore me."

- "I feel terrible when we fight and you stay mad at me."

- "I feel so sad that we have lost each other."

When hurts are expressed with energetic honesty (meaning that the words and the feeling state are resonant), a spouse will usually receive them with tenderness. As Marcia and I witness this in a mentoring session, we can see walls melt and often tears will well up in one or both partners. It is touching and sacred to behold.

9. Expressing remorse and personal responsibility.

The outright expression of remorse or sorrow is one of the most deeply intimate experiences a human can have. It rarely happens. Most often, the words "I'm sorry" are utilized as tools in a control pattern. If I don't want you to be mad at me, I will tell you "I'm sorry" as a form of damage control. In doing so, I am likely to squelch your attempt to express your anger or hurt. I not only prevent your feelings from being expressed, but I also attempt to avoid my own hurt at your criticisms. It is very easy to detect such verbalizations of sorrow as control patterns. Everything stagnates. This is the hallmark of a control pattern: stagnant emotional expression.

Real remorse has quite the opposite effect on the shared energy field. There is potent movement of energy between partners when one expresses true remorse. A profound release of blocked energy occurs when one spouse can acknowledge how sorry he is for how he has behaved.

Most adults confuse remorse with guilt. Energetically, they are very different. Guilt is directed toward oneself. It is most often experienced as self-blame. The body contracts and the mind conjures such statements as:

- "I really screwed up."

- "I feel stupid."

- "I can't believe I did it again."

- "You must hate me."

These statements reflect an energy turned inward and, as such, do not really lead to intimacy. Guilt is how I feel toward me; remorse is how I feel toward you. It is the recognition that I have truly impacted you in a negative way. It is entering into your world and knowing that I caused you suffering. Remorse is the empathy of the responsible heart. It is not just "feeling your pain;" it is the fully acknowledged, fully felt condition of knowing that I participated in the creation of your anguish. Remorse is the backbone of humility. It allows me to stand upright in mutual compassion for myself and for you.

In remorse, I am able to transcend life as a victim by my willingness to embrace the difficult truth that I am sometimes a victimizer. In our shared energy field, it hurts me that I hurt you. Our boundaries soften. To drop into my remorse is to release into the unbounded space of clear relationship. Its expression bridges the chasm between victim and victimizer and creates the opening for sorrow's soul sister, heartfelt forgiveness. Together, remorse and forgiveness create the energetic ecosystem where pure intimacy breeds openly.

There have been numerous books and articles written about forgiveness, but surprisingly few about remorse. Yet we believe that until we can enter into our remorse, forgiveness is a mask. We cannot really forgive somebody we think we are superior to, and if we think we have no remorse, then we are placing ourselves above our partner. Forgiveness under these conditions is a control pattern designed to keep us safe and superior. A precondition to forgiveness is the willingness to be fully affected by our partners. We must be open to the range of our feelings, including our remorse, before forgiveness can be authentic. A falsely spiritual kind of forgiveness is the outgrowth of emotional bypass surgery where feelings are antiseptically removed from relationship.

We reach this place of remorse when we are able to let go of all the ways we protect against taking responsibility. We release into our humility. When a spouse is ready for this, Marcia and I will encourage her to take the plunge with such statements as:

- "I'm so sorry I caused you to lose trust in me."
- "I know I've hurt you. I'm truly sorry."
- "I'm sorry for my mistakes."

- "I see how I have harmed you and I understand that it may be hard to forgive me."

- "I love you and it pains my heart to see how I have let you down."

There's profound movement in the shared energy field when such remorse is genuinely expressed. One other cautionary note can be seen in a couple I mentored with Marcia. When Connor says to his partner Carol, "If I upset you, then I'm sorry," he's still playing the control game. "If, then" statements suggest a weak sense of responsibility. Remorse is predicated on taking full responsibility for one's own part in a conflict or destructive engagement. "If I upset you" implies that I am not convinced that you are hurt. This is not real remorse. The will be no real release into vulnerability and connection without full responsibility.

10. Opening to mature need

As you will recall, immature need is experienced as demands that our partners be what we want them to be. They become the objects of our self-centered, childish expectations. Mature need is quite different. It is the substance and spirit of human relationship. Marriage is its breeding ground. In our long-term committed relationships, we can move beyond the fierce struggle for autonomy and surrender into deep appreciation for our partner's significance in our lives.

Mature need involves the full-bodied awareness of how much our partner adds to our life. From the place of our mature need, we say:

- "I don't want to live without you."

- "Meeting you is the best thing that ever happened to me."

- "I thank God you are in my life."

- "You matter so much to me."

- "I need you so much."

Such expression of need occurs when we have been able to drop our control patterns and enter into the space of our innocence. Often when partners attempt to say such things before they have released the more protective, charging emotions, the words are stiff and artificial. Only by loosening the resistance in the body will we allow ourselves to truly feel our mature need. Once we can do this, we discover that while we could survive without each other, we cannot fulfill our need for self-expression. Through our mature need, we are open to seeing our spouses more clearly. We can see them for the wondrous souls they really are. We know that our own lives are so much the better for their presence.

11. Expressing love, gratitude, and positive intent

As we come to the completion of our model of full self-expression, we access the source of all that is good. Love is at the core of our being, and it emanates outward in almost infinite variations of human expression. As John Pierrakos puts it, "Love is the force that unifies the two fundamental qualities of life—*energy* and *consciousness*." The gravitational pull of love draws us down into the center of our humanity, into a place where we can simultaneously reside in the separateness of our autonomy and the oneness of our connection. "I love you" is the declaration of this reality. Love is the connective tissue in the fabric of our relatedness.

After we have pumped up our chests, raised our voices, stomped our feet, and fueled our bodies with adrenaline-induced bravado; after we have released our firebrand feelings and brought forth our fears, hurts, and needs; after we have cleared the path to our sincere sorrow and the humility that it demands of us: only then we are awakened to the consciousness of our truest condition.

When love prevails through the flotsam and jetsam of our control patterns, myths, and hubristic denial of our limitations, we open up to our magnificence. We finally meet up with that elusive person we have been chasing all over Wonderland, like Alice after the White Rabbit. This is who we are! We should treasure this connection to our essential self, for it will fade. Fears and doubts will creep back in. And again we will need to move through layers of feeling. This is the steady truth of the human condition. There is no eternal bliss. But the process itself—expanding and contracting, charging and discharging—is the passionate theme of life.

When couples reach this stage in the full self-expression model, they are ready to let each other know how much they love and appreciate each other. We invite them to convey this with words such as:

- "I love you so much."

- "I love and appreciate your honesty and integrity."

- "I love that you listened so openly to all I had to share."

- "You are an amazing person. I love your laughter and you tears."

- "I appreciate how smart you are."

- "I have such gratitude for your courage and willingness to take risks."

- "I am your greatest fan. You inspire me to persevere when times are tough."

- "I cherish your sense of humor."

Sharing love and appreciation stokes the creative fires and paves the way for great things to unfold. No longer shackled by the energetic constraints of control patterns, couples have freed their energies to live life more adventurously and spontaneously.

Marriage Mentoring

o o o o o o o o o o o o o o o o o o o o o o o

If you should say, 'It is enough, I have reached perfection,' all is lost. For it is the function of perfection to make one know one's imperfection.

—Saint Augustine

This too is a function of relationship to know, honor, admit to, have compassion for, and live with one's (and another's) imperfections. When Marcia and I lead couples' retreats, fear saturates the room on the opening night. Couples sense that they are going to expose aspects of their hidden lives not only to the others in the room but to each other. The knowledge that we are imperfect creatures does not sit well with us. Our childhood conditioning robs us of our innate self-expression and leaves us fearing exposure. Couples have little desire to crack the control patterns and feel the "imperfect" emotions that lay beneath.

All of us in committed relationships are blinded by our control patterns. We cannot see what seems too risky to see. We strive for perfection so we don't have to experience the possibility of being hurt. On some fundamental level, most of us do not feel truly accepted because we don't believe we are acceptable. When, in childhood, we learn that our primary emotions are too intense, offensive, inappropriate, selfish, or dangerous, we diminish our spirit. Our innocent connection to our self-regulating emotional repertoire is severed. In

Chilton Pearce's words, "Cut off from our spirit, we spend the rest of our lives trying to prove our innocence."

"Marriage mentoring" is the name Marcia and I have given to our work with couples. It is designed to help couples establish what we call "mature innocence." This means being able to express the full range of human emotion with an awareness of the limits of each particular expression. In other words, we are innocent in our openness to express forbidden emotions and we are mature in recognizing that there is a greater reality and an abiding love that is the girding for all other emotions. In mentoring, couples are encouraged to bring vitality to their marriages by following the flow of shared energy. If the couple is faithful to the task, truly remarkable results are achieved.

In this final chapter, we will learn about how mentoring differs from conventional couples' therapy and what this means specifically for couples who choose to work on their relationship in this way. The process of mentoring is based on the conviction that the committed relationship is the ideal environment for the development of our human potential. We believe that couples are drawn together in order to encourage and challenge each other to exceed even their wildest expectations.

Marcia and I conceive of mentoring as an "experience-based" form of intervention; that is, the emphasis of the work is on the living experience of each moment. The greatest breakthroughs to truth and intimacy occur when couples embody, or inhabit, the present experience between each other. When spouses can relinquish their grip on story and myth, they meet each other in heart and soul. Experience is the bridge over the chasm of words, ideas, concepts and causal thinking.

In mentoring, each partner's narrative is woven into present experience in order to deepen connection. One person's story of betrayal can lead to a poignant moment of awareness, and expression of angry mistrust at his partner followed by her open-hearted willingness to receive the anger culminates in his heart cracking open in bittersweet love and pain for her acceptance of his truth. In mentoring, it is not insight that brings about change. It is the experience of long-denied emotions that leads to intimacy, connection, and the change that emerges from a liberation of life-force.

The flow of the work is simply a reversal of the separation process that each partner went through in their personal and relational development. At the dawn of our lives, each of us felt pure, embodied love (unless we were born into a hostile environment). This pure love was experienced as a full-bodied openness to the object of our intense affection and attachment. While not the equivalent of the mature love of an adult who is capable of empathy and altruism, it is absolute in its own right. In pure love, we hold nothing back. The loss of innocence is really the loss of pure love. In this state of love, we are exquisitely fragile. We can be radically rocked by any breach of relationship. Once we begin to experience the reality of separation from our love object and the awareness that there are limits to our connection, we are unceremoniously introduced to need.

Need is pure embodied love with a consciousness of its absence. So as we begin to appreciate the importance of relationship to our own survival and wholeness, we will feel need. The awareness of need can leave us feeling quite vulnerable. When, as children, our need for connection went unmet, we began to feel our primary restorative feelings of fear, anger, and hurt. When these feelings were disavowed by the adult world, we learned to control and hide them from ourselves and others. Thus, we recoiled back from pure embodied love, through the experience of unabashed need, into our primary feelings and ultimately into our adult control patterns, which get played out with nauseating routine in our marriages.

In the mentoring process, our goal is to take couples through their control patterns, into primary emotions, toward a realization of their mature need, and ultimately into pure embodied love with the added element of mature adult appreciation for who the other truly is. This, in a nutshell, is the aim of our mentoring work.

Mentoring differs from traditional couples counseling in a variety of ways:

- Mentoring is not about moving from dysfunctional to functional. It offers couples the opportunity to take the relationship into uncharted territories of pure embodied love, honesty, individual fulfillment, creative expression, and higher-intensity pleasure.

- Unlike classical behavioral couples' work, mentoring operates from the assumption that couples do not need to rehearse new behaviors or incorporate listening skills. Instead, relationships evolve organically as couples express themselves in a more direct and unfiltered way. Behaviors change naturally as couples become more honest.

- Strong emotions are considered essential to the mentoring process. Energy cannot be denied.

- Conventional couples' counseling emphasizes conflict resolution. Often conflict is viewed as dangerous and antithetical to healthy interaction. In mentoring, conflict is seen as the lifeblood of intimacy. Conflict that is expressed honestly allows for two strong people to draw from each other's differences.

- In mentoring, we view problems couples are having as information that tells us where they are in the process of relationship development. We use the problem to help us understand what is not being expressed rather than see the problem as something that needs to be fixed.

- In mentoring, couples are working with other couples who have "walked the talk." The mentors are people who have developed themselves and their relationships through devotion, hard work, and a willingness to continually grow.

- In mentoring, we recognize that all people become "embedded" in viewing life through their myths and narratives. The mentoring process is designed to help each partner make "perspective leaps," which liberate them from repetitious behaviors. These perspective leaps occur when couples are supported in fully experiencing the emotions that underlie their myths.

- Mentoring is an experience-based process. This means that in each session, couples are actively engaged in experiences that will help them break loose from habituated control patterns. They are not just sitting there discussing their relationship.

- In mentoring we use an approach that we call "catalyzing," which means that we prompt couples to express themselves in unfamiliar or uncomfortable ways. We serve as catalysts for couples to venture into uncharted emotional territory.

On this final point, a mentor's role is to help the couple express the unexpressed. Often they do not have the know-how or they have learned that it is taboo to express themselves in certain ways. It is the Voice of Judgment that turns genius children into conformist grownups. As adults, we edit out much of what flows through our emotional mind. The selfish, cruel, needy, arrogant, and vulnerable impulses that arise within generally remain in lockdown. Yet, there is a place for their expression. In catalyzing, we "feed" spouses expressions that appear to be lurking near the surface and interfering with deeper connection, so partners often benefit when they are given permission to express taboo sentiments. This is what we have already seen in the previous chapter on full self-expression. We include here a brief list of taboo expressions to provide a further understanding of what we mean.

Taboo Expressions

- "What about me!"
- "Don't leave."
- "I'll get you!"
- "Give it to me!"
- "My way!"

- "I want it all!"
- "You can't have it!"
- "You take care of it!"
- "I won't!"
- "I hate you!"
- "Help me."
- "I'm really scared."
- "I'm so angry!"
- "Please!" (begging)
- "I want to fuck you."
- "Would you play with me?"
- "Touch me."
- "That hurts."

How Mentoring Looks

Nathaniel and Lisa arrive for an initial session with Marcia and me. Both look at us—no, they look *to* us, desperate for help, even before a word is spoken. Immediately we ask them to look instead at each other. We ask them to breath and simply to be aware of what they feel and experience in this precise moment. We ask them to say aloud what is happening in the moment. Nathaniel tells Lisa, "You go first." She looks at him with a trace of frustration and a dash of disapproval. Then she talks about his unwillingness to come to the session. We remind her to stay with what she is experiencing in the moment, which she eventually gets to after three more attempts to talk about Nathaniel.

We have discovered that couples find it exceedingly difficult to stay in the flow of present experience, preferring instead to talk about their respective stories. Their respective descriptions of what is happening in their relationship are like two interpretations of an abstract painting. The narratives help us to get a sense of how each constructs reality and what control patterns they employ, but overall we do not wish to spend a great deal of time talking about the problems. Indeed, a big part of the problem is the story. By helping a couple to be aware of what is occurring within and between them in real time, they learn the primary tool to help guide them when they are not with us.

With Nathaniel and Lisa, we learn from their stories that she sees him as uncaring and somewhat irresponsible and he sees her as hyper-controlling and perfectionist. Both come across as hardened and critical. Neither reveals tenderness. They both claim that they love the other, but it cannot be felt by either Marcia or myself. We understand this to mean not that they are lying, but that the love is concealed behind very constricting control patterns and myths. Their bodies are literally contracted and in full protection mode.

If we let them, they will engage in an endless circular debate about who is right. They can really get on a roll. There is lots of energy, but it leads nowhere. It seems to us that the only way they are able to remain in some form of contact is through blame. There is clearly a charge in their debating, but it only carries them so far.

In our work with them, it is not our goal to get either of them to change. Instead, we want invite them more fully into the conflict and let the energy of it carry them to deeper levels of feeling and experiencing. First, we help them frame the problem more clearly, as they now see it from a cause-and-effect perspective. Nathaniel says, "If you would lighten up and stop being so driven, I would be more open to you and want to support you." Lisa counters, "If you would just do the things that need to get done, then I could relax and be more pleasant." It's clear that they both have a strong allegiance to their respective narratives. We encourage them to really feel the strength of conviction they each have.

Then, each begins to hint at the negativity they harbor toward each other when they don't get what they want. We ask them to bring this more into the light of day. Nathaniel reveals that he wants to punish Lisa by withholding affection. He secretly wants her to fail at all those endeavors that occupy so much of her time. Lisa opens up and says she wants to make Nathaniel feel inadequate by not being able to keep up with her, and she likes to keep him in fear that she would leave if he doesn't shape up. We don't have them merely confess these private negative intentions to us but energetically express them directly to each other. It is difficult to convey through the written word how crucial it is for spouses to release the charge of destructive energy that otherwise foments and comes through in more insidious ways.

"You First"

Childhood needs, as mentioned earlier are the secret demands each partner has of the other to fulfill the early life requirements for protection and connection. From our childhood need, we want our partner to do the work for us. We learn from Nathaniel that he grew up with a mother who lacked warmth and was critical of any display of weakness. From Lisa we find out that her father was cruel; no matter what she did, it was never good enough. When he died, even though she took care of him until death, she discovered he left her one single dollar in his will.

Consequently, Nathaniel's immature need is for Lisa to shower him with warmth and affection without him having to ask for it. Lisa's immature need is to be admired, appreciated, and fully accepted by Nathaniel, also without having to let on that she craves it. These childhood needs are in essence fantasies we have of our partners to be the all-good, all-knowing, all-loving, perfect parent. While we know that these needs are unrealistic on an "adult" level, nevertheless they remain powerful, behind-the-scenes demands. In Nathaniel's fantasy, Lisa would greet him upon his arrival home with soft, nurturing energy and undivided attention. Her fantasy is that he has no needs of her (unlike her demanding, ungrateful father) and that he sweeps her off her feet and protects her from all harm. When they express these immature needs to each other (which we encourage them to do with as much passion as possible), we can feel the tension between them dissipate.

Later in our work, we learn how terrifying it is for Lisa to let go of her Super Woman persona because she lacks trust in all men and has convinced herself that Nathaniel is no exception. Under the spell of her myth, she marginalizes all the ways that Nathaniel has exhibited trustworthiness and exaggerates the ways he's let her down. By expressing her fears, she begins to see that he listens and accepts her. Thus she starts to get her mature needs for contact met. This is a fundamental axiom of our model: Whenever unmet childhood needs are brought out of the closet, the likelihood that mature needs for empathic connection will get met increases. Subsequently, Lisa moves into rage and grief at her dad, and we have her release this intense energy physically. We also have Nathaniel "protect" her by himself directing anger toward her father in "role play" fashion and saying that he won't let him hurt her anymore. Thus they begin to ally with their common feelings rather than alienate each other.

With Nathaniel, we soon discover that he is scared of Lisa's judgments and compensates by acting uncaring. He learned long ago to cut off from how hurt he felt by his mother's emotional rejection, and he repeats the control pattern of avoidance with Lisa. The truth is, he gets easily hurt by her and, in our work, he starts to express that hurt more readily, without the accusatory energy that previously characterized his communication. In mentoring, we know that each partner is biologically wired toward self-preservation as the immediate, first-order need. Nathaniel's accusatory tone reflects his "fight or flight" reaction to Lisa's harsh energy. As he releases the charged energy of this place, he literally softens into a less defended expression of hurt.

One way we get him to release his charge is to amplify and focus his accusations. So instead of saying, "I sometimes think you just can't change," we ask him to express it like this: "I hate that you keeping going until you drop. It stresses me out and makes me just want to scream." Embedded in his original expression is the implication that if she can't change, he doesn't want to be with her. When he openly and passionately owns that he gets angry, he then can let go and make fuller contact with the primary feeling of hurt. When he comes at her with statements like "I sometimes think that you just can't change" he is conveying a message of despair. This is a defeated, dispirited energy that chokes the life force out of the relationship. Marcia and I encouraged him to clearly express his fear about staying in the relationship rather than send Lisa encoded, foreboding messages. When he was able to express this fear more openly, he could connect it to the helplessness he felt around his mom, and the real grief associated with it.

Simple, basic shifts in expression such as that just noted with Nathaniel go a long way with most couples. Standard mentoring suggestions we make to couples include:

- Having the couple stand rather than sit
- Raising the decibel level of their communication
- Altering distance and proximity
- Stripping away the smoke and mirrors in their arguments and having them give clear voice to what they are implying ("I'm right, you're wrong," "My way!")
- Switching sides and arguing with equal vehemence
- Charging the undercharged partner and discharging the overcharged
- Using music to encourage a drop into an emotion that is percolating but still resisted

- Uncovering the disguised "I want" behind every complaint
- Having one partner express an emotion the other struggles with in "expression by proxy"

There are many more options, and really the limit lies with the creativity of the mentors and the people they mentor. With Lisa, we found that to uncover what she wants from Nathaniel and to ask for it rather than to complain afterward was both difficult and profoundly important for her to do. Lisa was loathe to need Nathaniel and exhibited a control pattern of acting very disappointed after he "let her down." Her disappointment was in truth feigned, because in order to truly feel it she would have to allow herself to want him. The soft place of real disappointment remained inside the cement overcoat of judgment.

Verbal Misdirection

Couples will often use certain feeling words to misdirect each other from the more difficult primary emotion. "I'm disappointed, surprised, hurt, worried, angry, or sorry" can all mean something quite different than they suggest. Sometimes, the more therapy a couple has had, the craftier they become at utilizing feeling words to control against actually feeling. Since many therapies do not openly encourage the expression of feelings right there in the office, clients easily learn to talk about feelings while rarely experiencing them. (Even utilizing such terms as "office" and "client" may be a subtle and unconscious way that therapists discourage emotion.)

For Lisa to even begin to entertain that she needed Nathaniel was initially far too risky. She was clever enough to quickly learn to say, "Of course I need Nathaniel," but she was no where near truly feeling it. Her complaints held a charge that helped her experience herself as autonomous. When she was able to make the connection that each complaint was associated with a want, that "You never initiate sex" also meant "I want to know if you still find me desirable," she was able for the first time to experience a need that she long ago disowned.

Lisa needed to remain in her charged energy of complaining for quite a while until she could open to her desire to make Nathaniel feel bad. Once she could take ownership of lower-self energy, she could then finally release into more vulnerable feelings, including her need for Nathaniel. Marcia and I believe that those who have been victimized as children can never move past the identification with the collapsed and defeated self until they can experience the destructive current within themselves. It is not enough to just express rage at the perpetrator; a survivor will need to contact her "inner perpetrator." When Lisa does this, she no longer needs to split off good and bad and bequeath the bad to Nathaniel. She then can begin to feel how important he is.

Between the two of them, they had become so adept at creating the white noise of accusation that they could no longer notice how truly affected they are by each other. When couples are mired in cause-and-effect consciousness, they overlook the reverberating interactions of layered emotions. The energy squirts out as reciprocal blame but never gets expressed in its entirety. When Nathaniel begins to see for the first time that Lisa needs him and that she really misses him when he checks out, his heart opens to her, and he can begin to feel real remorse for his control pattern. No longer can he justify his coldness as a rightful reaction to her behavior.

As Lisa and Nathaniel realize and reveal how affected they are by each other, they open the floodgates of warmth and appreciation. There is no doubt that they love each other, and as they could once again touch the love, they seemed to transform. Each was lighter, funnier, and more inspired. It was clear to us how they had moved from self-preservation consciousness (protection) to creative self-expression. Of course, exceptional couples will vacillate between their contracted state of control patterns and expansive self-expression, but many others never realize the second option.

Expression by proxy

In a shared energy field, it is often unclear where an emotion originates. Frequently the withheld energy of one partner boils over and out through the other. Each one of us brings to our relationships long-denied feelings from our childhood. In our mentoring, Marcia and I often find it valuable to have spouses support each other in expressing emotions that were invalidated or avoided early in life. What gets directed toward a spouse is often an emotion that was locked down toward a parent.

In another example of a couple we mentored, Gil and Mary Ann fell into a control pattern where she would criticize and he would constantly seek approval. When it came out that Gil's mother was hyper-critical and shaming, we encouraged him to express his anger at her during a mentoring session. He had tremendous difficulty doing this. So we asked Mary Ann to express the anger for him. As she shouted at his mom, expressing all that he feared to reveal, he began to feel relief and had the added benefit of being touched by how Mary Ann "protected" him. This is what Marcia and I call expression by proxy. It takes emotional energy that is withheld by one partner and consciously releases it through the other, who has more access to it. Expression by proxy can be an extremely effective way for couples to utilize their shared energy and learn to ally with each other over something that historically became a wedge between them. Through channeling the raw power available in every relationship, mentoring helps couples to come alive.

The Big Picture

Our hope is that all committed couples have a chance to discover their great potential. Couples become alienated and devitalized when they learn to reject important aspects of who they are. It is a false maturity to be always reasonable and polite. In an exceptional relationship, manners and etiquette are unnecessary. We will treat each other magnificently when we learn to be real, not when we memorize rules. Pure love exists at the far end of full emotional expression. Our hearts burst open with empathy, delight, attraction, appreciation, excitation, and wonder when we are able to express that which we long ago learned was too dangerous.

Secreted within our childhood needs are innocent fantasies of knights in shining armor and princesses who will cherish and adore us. Can we bestow upon these childhood needs their rightful place in our relationships? Behind every negative and destructive impulse is a wound that was never allowed to heal. Can we see that our rage is not our essence so that we can humbly acknowledge its presence? Inside every fear is a profound need for soulful connection. Can we stop pretending we are beyond being scared and reach out for a little comfort? Attached to every control pattern is a stern admonishment against the overt expression of our fears, hurts and angers. Can we learn to turn to our most loved one and expose these emotional truths? That we can all do these things with our partners, this is our hope for all of you.

We have become a culture of reticent relationships. As odd as it sounds, most of us have forgotten how to live in our bodies. We engage primarily from the neck up with infrequent forays into sexual and emotional contact. The Exceptional Marriage is an embodied experience of connection and expression. Love is not a mindset—it is an erasure of all the controls we place on our experience of full connection. We cannot compartmentalize love, as in, "I will love you with my heart but not with my pelvis." To love means to feel it all.

Full, embodied love is the ultimate mark of the Exceptional Marriage. Exposure to this place helps each one of us become unbounded. The expansive, creative, pulsating, vibrant energy that is released is then available in raising phenomenal children or healing an ailing planet. Marriage falls short of its divine purpose when it remains in safety mode. By reclaiming the full embodied experience of love that is the child's birthright and coupling it with the wisdom of a conscious, mature adult, we can manifest everything that this planet and its inhabitants so desperately need.

We explore the inner reaches of our humanity through commitment to another. It is a rich and fruitful exploration that knows no end. This type of work can reap broad dividends as marriage partners learn to bring out the greatness in each other. Too often the energy of relationship is desiccated by mutual avoidance of potent life force. Every marriage is capable of becoming a force of nature. When we learn to embrace the intensity of life within and between us, when we choose to move toward rather than away from our partners as conflict arises, when we can wake up to the absolute, breathless wonder of the possibilities in store for us, we can rock the universe.

Marriage is the foundation relationship upon which our ability to experience pure embodied love rests. This is a love that is not divided into parts (affection, filial, erotic, empathic, maternal, devotional, philanthropic). It is a love that is felt fully and completely—heart, soul and pelvis. The creative fires that leap from this energy can alter the world it ways we have yet to imagine. For couples to bring to a world in need of emotional liberation the fruits of their own miraculous journey is the ultimate purpose of radical commitment. This is the big picture. This is going all the way.

If you would like to join the growing network of couples who are committed to becoming exceptional, please visit us at http://www.exceptionalmarriage.com/.

Afterword

Marcia and I thought long and hard about using the term Exceptional Marriage to describe and convey our vision. We felt it was important to end this book with a brief explanation of our reasoning. So, here goes.

As you may have figured out by now, we are firmly convinced that long-term commitment offers opportunities for growth as a conscious human being that are not easily found elsewhere. The culture at large sends us widely disparate messages. On the one hand, we are all taught that marriage is the culmination of healthy adult development. Most young adults face some serious pressure to hurry up and get married. On the other hand, nearly everything that happens post-nuptials works against success in relationship. Most couples feel extremely isolated and that they are in uncharted territory when it comes to the deep emotions that intimacy requires. In a society that favors productivity over spontaneity, most relationships aspire to little else than healthy functioning. They cannot afford to take risks that could possibly force them to deviate from the established path.

We use the term "exceptional" because such couples are willing to break the rules of engagement that champion functionality and productivity over creativity and passion. An Exceptional Marriage shakes up the status quo. It changes the operational definition of marriage as a business arrangement. It is our hope that more and more couples will use their relationships as the birthplace of magnificence and the ground for inspiration.

We also have quite consciously chosen to use the term "marriage" because it holds such power. We are well aware that many gay and lesbian couples are not offered the same rights to a legal marriage as heterosexuals. However, we strongly believe that the quality of a committed relationship is not determined by gender but by the choices people make. We know of many same-sex couples who long for the legal right to marry and who can and do marry through a variety of religious and spiritual organizations. Their "marriages" are equally valid in our eyes and hearts. The difficulties same-sex couples face in staying together in a culture that does not sanction their relationships goes far beyond what straight couples have to face. Thus we use the word marriage not to exclude anyone but to embrace all. It is our sincere desire to support all couples, gay and straight, in attaining an Exceptional Marriage.

Bibliography

de Quincey, Christian. 2005. *Radical Knowing*. South Paris, ME. Park Street Press

Eigen, Michael. 1996. *Psychic Deadness*. Northvale, N.J. Aronson

Gray, John. 2002. *What You Feel You Can Heal*. Vermilion County, Il. Vermilion

Gleason, Brian. 2001. *Mortal Spirit*. Lincoln, Nebraska iUniverse

Grothe, Mardy. PhD. 2004. *Oxymoronica*. New York, N.Y. Harper Collins

Johnson, S. M., EdD. 1996. The Practice of Emotionally Focused Couple Therapy: *Creating Connection*. New York, N.Y. Bruner/Mazel

Keen, Sam. 1983. The Passionate Life. San Francisco, CA. Harper Collins

Leonard, George. 1992. *Mastery*. New York, N.Y. Plume

McKibben, Bill. March/April 2007. *Reversal of Fortune*. Mother Jones Magazine

O'Murchu, Diarmuid. 1998. *Reclaiming Spirituality*. New York, N.Y. Crossroad

Pearce, Joseph. Chilton. 2002. *The Biology of Transcendence*. Rochester VT. Park Street Press

Perel, Esther. 2006. *Mating in Captivity*. New York, N.Y. Harper Collins

Pierrakos, John. 1987. Core Energetics. Mendicino CA. LifeRhthym.

Reich, Wilhelm. 1973. *The Function of the Orgasm*. New York, N.Y. Farrar, Straus and Garoux

Rosen, Julie. 1988. *Going Ape*. Chicago, Il. Contemporary Books

Rosenthal, Norman E. 2002. *The Emotional Revolution*. New York, N.Y. Citadel Press

Szaz, Thomas. 1974. *The Myth of Mental Illness: Foundations of a Theory of Personal Conduct*. New York, N.Y. Harper & Row

Senge, Peter., O. Scharmer, J. Jaworski, B. S. Flowers. 2005. *Presence*. New York, N.Y. Currency Doubleday

Schnarch, David. 1991. *Constructing the Sexual Crucible*. New York, N.Y. Norton

Siegel, Daniel. 1999. *The Developing Mind*. New York, N.Y. Guilford

Viorst, Judith. 2003. *Grown Up Marriage*. New York, N.Y. Free Press

Wile, Daniel. B. 1993. *Couples Therapy: A Nontraditional Approach*. New York, N.Y. Wiley-Interscience

About The Authors

Brian and Marcia Gleason have been a married couple since 1978. Brian is a licensed Clinical Social Worker and is a senior faculty member of the Institute of Core Energetics in New York. He leads workshops, teaches and trains internationally. Brian has also authored a book on transpersonal psychology entitled Mortal Spirit. Marcia is also a licensed Clinical Social Worker. She is a graduate of the Institute of Core Energetics and a certified Life Coach. Marcia trains couples, has a private practice, and has taught internationally.

978-0-595-45151-7
0-595-45151-9

Made in the USA
Lexington, KY
08 January 2013